# Learn
# LIBRARY OF CONGRESS
# SUBJECT ACCESS

## INTERNATIONAL EDITION

## Lynn Farkas

TotalRecall Publications, Inc..
1103 Middlecreek
Friendswood, Texas 77546
281-992-3131    281-482-5390 Fax
www.totalrecallpress.com

Copyright © 2016 Lynn Farkas
Based on the original works by Jacki Ganendran and Lynn Farkas

ISBN:  978-1-59095-439-3
UPC:  6-43977-44394-6
Printed in the United States of America with simultaneous printing in Australia, Canada, and United Kingdom.

FIRST INTERNATIONAL EDITION, JANUARY 2016
1   2   3   4   5   6   7   8   9   10


Library of Congress Control Number:  2016935554

# Table of Contents

# Preface

*Learn Library of Congress subject access* covers the skills necessary for a subject cataloger in a library or information agency, whether at a professional or a paraprofessional level. It is suitable for use by librarianship students, and for those studying subject cataloging by themselves as part of their continuing professional development. Since most catalogs provide some subject access, it is important for all library students and most library staff to be familiar with at least the basics of subject cataloging.

This book introduces students to the concepts of subject analysis and subject description. It provides practical guidance on identifying important topics and allocating appropriate terms to describe them. Since *Library of Congress subject headings* (LCSH) is the most widely used subject headings list worldwide, the main focus of the book is on effectively using this scheme. A mastery of Library of Congress subject headings will assist catalogers using any subject headings scheme.

This first international edition of *Learn Library of Congress subject access* builds on previous Australian and North American editions, with a broader range of exercises and more information on chronological, geographic and name headings. A new chapter explains the features of Library of Congress' online product, *Classification Web*, and how it can be used for efficiently searching LCSH.

Throughout the text there are exercises to practise and test new skills, with answers for self-checking at the back of the book. You may not always agree completely with the answers given, and it is useful to check them with a teacher or experienced cataloger. Always bear in mind that there is often room for more than one interpretation or emphasis, particularly in the area of subject analysis.

LCSH is continually updated to include new concepts and incorporate revisions to existing headings. Answers to exercises reflect current practices as recorded in the 37th (2015) edition *of Library of Congress subject headings* and the online version of the *Subject headings manual.* Your answers may vary slightly if other editions of the scheme are used. Throughout the text, references have been made to relevant sections of the *Subject headings manual* by way of the section numbers—e.g., Free-Floating Subdivisions (H 1095).

## Note on Spelling and Capitalization

This book is used in North America, Europe and Australasia, across countries that employ different spelling conventions for English words. For consistency, American spelling has been adopted for the text.

Titles included in the text are capitalized according to standard library cataloging practice—that is, apart from names, only the first word of the title has a capital letter. This is intended to accustom library students and staff to this style.

# CHAPTER ONE
## Introduction to Subject Cataloging

### Introduction

Cataloging is the preparation of bibliographic information for catalog records, using a set of cataloging tools that are the agreed international rules and standards.

Cataloging consists of:
- descriptive cataloging
- subject cataloging
- classification.

This workbook focuses on subject cataloging. Other workbooks in the *Learn Library Skills Series* cover descriptive cataloging (*Learn Cataloging the RDA Way*) and classification (*Learn Dewey Decimal Classification edition 23* and *Learn Library of Congress Classification*).

### Subject Cataloging

Subject cataloging is the process of determining subject headings for an item. The cataloger seeks the headings that best represent the topics of the work in words and/or phrases given in an authoritative list. Subject headings:
- cover the main topic of the work, and also other important themes or aspects
- allow multiple subject headings to be assigned to a work
- provide additional access points for finding information (and so complement and supplement the classification number and author/title access points)
- are used primarily for remote searching (i.e., via a catalog) to discover similar items.

### Aims of Subject Cataloging

- to provide access by subject to all relevant materials
- to bring together all references to material on the same subject regardless of different terminology, different subject approaches, and the changing nature of the material itself
- to provide a formal description of the subject content of the item in the most precise terms possible, whether this be a word, phrase, class number etc.
- to show affiliations among subject fields
- to provide access through a vocabulary common to any considerable group of users
- to provide subject entry at any level of analysis
- to provide subject access to materials through all suitable principles of subject organization—i.e., matter, process, application

- to provide the means for the user to select from among all items in any particular category—e.g., most recent.

 **EXERCISE 1.1**

1.  What is your understanding of a

    a) Subject:

    b) Subject heading:

2.  Write down as many subject headings lists as you can:

## Who Uses Subject Headings Lists?
- The cataloger or indexer—to allocate headings
- The searcher—to plan a search strategy—that is, to identify appropriate headings for use in searching for a particular topic. A searcher may be a library user or library staff
- The originator of the document (ideally) in order to use standard terminology.

 **EXERCISE 1.2**
*What needs do the following users have of a subject headings list?*

1.  Cataloger:

2.  Reference advisor:

3.  Library user:

4.  Acquisitions officer:

5.  Interlibrary loans officer:

6.  Author:

## Principles of Subject Cataloging

### Aboutness

First and foremost, subject cataloging should describe what a resource is about. Main concepts and substantial minor concepts should be identified and noted.

### User needs

The subject cataloger should always consider users and their needs. The heading, in wording and structure, should be one that the user would be most likely to look for.

### Uniform headings

Try to ensure uniform headings. All items dealing with one subject should be placed under the same heading.

**Terminology**

The aim is always to match the user's term with the heading in the catalog. Several problems arise, since you must choose among:

- synonyms
- variant spellings
- English vs other languages
- technical vs popular terms
- obsolete vs current terms
- homonyms.

**Direct entry**

Ideally, identify a heading that directly describes the subject:

 Cats

    *not*

    Mammals—Domestic animals—Cats

 **EXERCISE 1.3**

*Investigate the subject headings you would use to find information on the following topics.*

*Use two different types of libraries. Try to select two libraries that serve different clientele, for example a secondary school library and a tertiary academic library, or a public library and a special library. Make a note if you are unable to find any material on a topic in your library of choice. Why might this be?*

| | Topic | Library 1 | Library 2 |
|---|---|---|---|
| 1. | National parks in Canada | _____ | _____ |
| 2. | Building in tropical conditions | _____ | _____ |
| 3. | Smoking and health | _____ | _____ |
| 4. | Library classification schemes | _____ | _____ |
| 5. | Fitting a jacket | _____ | _____ |
| 6. | Women in business | _____ | _____ |

7.  Desktop publishing

8.  Marketing your
    services

9.  The Second World War

10. Cataloging non-book
    materials

11. Presentation skills for
    new teachers

12. Australian
    photographers

## Vocabulary Control

Subject catalogers strive to describe the topics of resources in a consistent manner. This involves using the same term all the time to indicate the same concept. It may also involve using a controlled list of terms (a thesaurus) to help catalogers identify and avoid synonyms or homonyms for that concept. Vocabulary control is the process of ensuring that terms are used to describe subjects consistently in a catalog, bibliography or index.

### Homonyms

A homonym is a word that sounds the same as another, but has a different meaning. Homonyms can be identified by checking dictionaries—homonyms will have different definitions for each of their usages.

### EXERCISE 1.4

*Provide two possible meanings for each of the following terms:*

| Term | Meanings |
|------|----------|
| 1. slack | 1. |
| | 2. |
| 2. slam | 1. |
| | 2. |
| 3. toast | 1. |
| | 2. |

| 4. | lag | 1. _____ |
| | | 2. _____ |
| 5. | cuff | 1. _____ |
| | | 2. _____ |

## Synonyms

A synonym is a word that has the same meaning as another. Synonyms can be identified by using dictionaries to define the words, or consulting general thesauri that group words with similar meanings together.

## EXERCISE 1.5

*Provide synonyms for the following words or phrases:*

| Term | Synonym/s |
|------|-----------|
| 1. author | _____ |
| 2. stamp collecting | _____ |
| 3. car | _____ |
| 4. monograph | _____ |
| 5. trailer | _____ |
| 6. serial | _____ |
| 7. hiking | _____ |
| 8. saturated | _____ |
| 9. slack | _____ |
| 10. corpulence | _____ |
| 11. elevators | _____ |
| 12. hirsute | _____ |
| 13. shore | _____ |
| 14. rage | _____ |
| 15. hemp | _____ |

**Controlled vocabulary**

A controlled vocabulary uses a set of predetermined terms to represent concepts. Only one term or phrase describes each concept; alternatives such as synonyms or variant spellings are not acceptable.

A controlled vocabulary identifies synonymous terms and selects one preferred term:

    Capsicum
        Use: Peppers

It establishes the size or scope of each topic:

    Baseball
        includes the concept softball

For homonyms, it explicitly identifies the multiple concepts expressed by that word or phrase:

    Springs (mechanical devices)
            vs
        Springs (water sources)

A controlled vocabulary can also record the hierarchical and associative relations of a concept. This type of controlled subject list is also called a **thesaurus**:

    Painting
        Broader term: Art
        Narrower term: Watercolor painting
        Related term: Drawing

*Library of Congress subject headings* (LCSH) is one example of a controlled vocabulary.

**Uncontrolled vocabulary**

An uncontrolled vocabulary uses the actual words in a document as an access point. It is also referred to as natural language, keyword or free text vocabulary. Uncontrolled vocabulary terms may be selected from the text or the title.

    **EXERCISE 1.6**

1.   List examples of systems that use

    a)   Controlled vocabulary:

    a)   Uncontrolled vocabulary:

2.    What are the advantages and disadvantages of controlled and uncontrolled
      vocabulary?

> *Controlled vocabulary*
> Advantages:
>
>
>
>
> Disadvantages:
>
>
>
>
>
> *Uncontrolled vocabulary*
> Advantages:
>
>
>
>
>
> Disadvantages:

## Pre-coordinate and Post-coordinate Indexing
### Pre-coordination
In a pre-coordinate system, the parts of a heading are put together (pre-coordinated) by the cataloger or indexer to create a specific subject heading. Terms are put together in a specific pre-determined order.

To retrieve documents from the system, the searcher must use the same terms in the search strategy. This requires the searcher to put together the heading in the same form as constructed by the cataloger. At the very least, the searcher needs to know what the subject heading begins with.

*Library of Congress subject headings* is a pre-coordinate system.

 In LCSH, for example,
    *Title*       Laws concerning the transporting of coal in Australia
    *Heading*   Coal—Transportation—Law and legislation—Australia

In a pre-coordinate system, there is no opportunity for the searcher to combine concepts in a search at the retrieval stage (although some retrieval systems, whose search capabilities allow each part of the subject heading to be accessed, can act in a 'post-coordinate' way).

**Post-coordination**
In a post-coordinate system, the cataloger may use several terms to cover all subjects. The searcher can then search using Boolean operators (and, not, or) to construct the search. The searcher need not be aware of all the terms used and there is no order of terms involved.

 *Title*        Laws concerning the transporting of coal in Australia
    *Headings*  Coal
                Laws *or* Legislation
                Transport *or* Transporting *or* Transportation
                Australia

The searcher will find this item by using any (or any combination) of the subject terms.

Most library catalogs use pre-coordinated subject headings. Many indexing services use post-coordination. The principles of subject cataloging remain the same, however, regardless of the indexing system used.

# CHAPTER TWO
# Subject Analysis

## Subject Analysis

Subject analysis is the process of deciding what a work is about.

Subject analysis involves several steps:
1. First, examine the work in hand to determine its content.
2. Identify the main topics or concepts covered, as well as related or subordinate subjects.
3. Decide what information is important to highlight. These will be the subjects you will record in your cataloging.
4. Then decide on several keywords that could represent these subjects.
5. Transfer the keywords into appropriate terminology (in this workbook, that terminology will be the *Library of Congress subject headings* (LCSH) scheme).
6. Using the keywords as a starting point, go to each term in the LCSH list to identify appropriate headings.

## Determining Content

To successfully analyze the subject of a work, it is important that you understand what the work is about. Catalogers do not have the time or the resources to read every work they deal with; instead they use a number of techniques to help them identify the main points the author is making. These include skimming, scanning and summarizing techniques.

***Skimming techniques*** involve examining the document for its structure and an overview of its contents. In journal articles, reports, and other short documents, look at the following:
- Title, subheadings, chapter headings
- First few paragraphs
- First paragraph of each subheading/section, OR
- Opening sentence of each paragraph
- Conclusion/summary paragraph, OR
- Last few paragraphs

In books or longer documents, look at the following:
- Title, subtitle
- Dust jacket notes or overview of work on back cover
- Foreword, preface, introduction
- Table of contents
- First chapter or chapters
- Concluding chapter, OR
- Summary remarks in final chapter

**Scanning techniques** involve examining the document for its main points. In both books and articles, look at the following:

- Pull quotes and italics (more common in articles)
- Point listings
- Key phrases
- 'This work describes . . . '   • 'We aim to . . . '
- 'The main point . . . '   • 'The research shows . . . '
- 'Key issues . . . '   • 'It was found that . . . '
- 'In summary . . . '

**Summarizing** involves paraphrasing the main points identified through skimming and scanning, to state what the item is about in a few sentences. This is also known as abstracting.

### EXERCISE 2.1

*Choose the statement that best expresses the main idea of the following paragraphs. More than one answer in each group may be correct.*
*You are not trying to find the correct answer but the best answer.*

1. The writing of political comments on walls seems to me to be justified, as long as they contain messages that would not otherwise reach the people, and as long as the writers of these comments have no regular access to other media such as newspapers or television. I only wish, though, that they would confine their aerosol activities to walls, and stop defacing public monuments and statues.

   The writer approves of political graffiti only if they
   a. attack the government
   b. are written so that everyone can understand them
   c. do not compete with the media (e.g., the press and television)
   d. contain useful or important information that people normally wouldn't see.

2. Most of us lead unhealthy lives: we spend far too much time sitting down. If, in addition, we are careless about our diets, our bodies soon become flabby and our systems sluggish. Then the guilt feelings start: 'I must go on a diet', 'I must try to lose weight', 'I must get more fresh air and exercise', 'I must stop smoking', 'I must try to keep fit'. There are some aspects of our unhealthy lives that we cannot avoid. I am thinking of such features of modern urban life as pollution, noise, rushed meals and stress. But keeping fit is a way to minimize the effects of these evils.

   Learning how to unwind can also improve our lifestyles. Yoga, as practised in the West, is the most widely known and popular of the systems for achieving the necessary state of relaxation. Contrary to popular belief, you do not have to learn a lot of strange words or become a Buddhist in order to benefit from Yoga. It seems ironical, though, that as our lives have improved in a material sense, we have found it increasingly necessary to go back to forms of activity—physical effort on the one hand, and relaxation on the other—that were the natural way of our forefathers.

Unfitness is the result of
a.   lack of fresh air and exercise
b.   overeating, smoking and living in towns
c.   not eating properly and not getting enough exercise
d.   not taking part in sports.

Pollution, noise and stress are examples of
a.   causes of unfitness
b.   bad features of living in towns
c.   the things we must avoid if we are to stay healthy
d.   industrial life and work.

Our reaction to being out of condition is to
a.   give up smoking and go on a diet
b.   start a programme of keep-fit exercises
c.   make resolutions to lead a healthier life
d.   take up a sport.

Many people believe that in order to practise yoga
a.   you must learn a new language
b.   you must become a Buddhist
c.   you must learn to relax completely
d.   you must wear special clothing.

Our forefathers were healthy because
a.   their way of life involved both exercise and relaxation
b.   they were careful to get plenty of fresh air and keep fit
c.   they lived in the country and spent time out of doors
d.   they had simple work to do and very little to worry about.

3.   List 4-5 keywords that describe important concepts/ideas/points contained in the passage for Question 2.

4.   Summarize the passage in one sentence.

## Determining Subjects

First, examine the item to decide on topics. You should make this decision based on the evidence in the work in hand, not on what you know or think about the topic. Then, find correct headings to describe the topics.

To decide on topics, examine the following for print resources, or equivalent categories for non-print material:

- title — may or may not be helpful
- subtitle — is often more useful
- author — may provide an indication of the broad topic if the author has published previously in the subject area
- foreword, preface, introduction — usually state the author's intention
- publisher — may give an indication if the publisher specializes in a particular subject area
- series — may be useful as an overall indication of broad subject matter
- table of contents, illustrations, index — are usually good indicators of the main topics
- text — can be used to confirm your ideas about the subject. Skim and scan the text and/or read a sample
- cataloging-in-publication — useful but use with care, as CIPs are prepared prior to publication, often without the work in hand.

   Look at the following example:

# When
# Your Partner
# Dies

*Mary Mortimer*

Hale & Iremonger

(title page)

# Contents

# Preface

I have written this book in an attempt to make sense of the two major tragedies in my life—the deaths of two partners, each of whom I loved deeply. These deaths, and that of a dear friend, are my main personal experiences of bereavement. I have therefore focused on the death of a partner, although I am strongly aware of the devastation which can result from the death of a parent or a child.

When we lose a parent, and especially both parents, we lose the generation 'above' us, the source of our life, our early knowledge of the world, so many of our characteristics and attitudes.

When our child dies, at whatever age, we are stunned by the unnatural order of events. We do not expect to survive our children: our hopes are for their future, even more than our own.

With the death of a partner, on the other hand, we lose the person who shares our everyday life, who is there for breakfast and dinner, with whom we share a home, a bed, many of our hopes and fears, memories and future plans. So the loss affects every aspect of our lives, and requires the most pervasive practical and emotional adjustments.

There are other books which present a more academic or professional approach to bereavement. I have written from my own experience—

and that of close friends whose grief I have shared. I have been able to draw conclusions about the common aspects of grieving, and the different effects of sudden and of expected death. I try to offer practical suggestions for dealing with situations you may not yet have encountered.

Since I am a very practical person, and control over my life is of great importance to me, I emphasise what can be <u>done</u> in coping with the loss of a partner and its aftermath. You may find it easier than I did to let things happen, to accept this massive disruption to your physical and emotional life. I hope, however, that you will find my descriptions of events and feelings reassuring and helpful. One of our most valuable sources of support in times of crisis is knowing that our experience is not unique, and that others have felt or behaved in a similar way.

For most couples who are still together, one will have to live through and beyond the death of the other. Yet death is perhaps the last remaining taboo. Not only do we not talk about it, we don't even call it by name. We prefer to say that 'the deceased' or the 'dearly departed' or the 'loved one' has 'passed away', 'gone', 'left us', 'gone to Heaven', is 'at rest' or 'at peace';  we talk around the event without using the words. By not naming death and dying, we deny the reality and make it more difficult for those who are close to it to share and express their sadness, their anxiety and their anger.

Many people who have no personal experience of death and loss, feel inadequate when a friend is bereaved. In their embarrassment they try to ignore this momentous event, and in so doing they add to their friend's feelings of hurt and isolation.

If you believe in a God or gods, and a life after death, I am sure it can be a great source of comfort and strength. I hope you do not turn away from your belief in your anger and feeling of betrayal. 'Why me?' is a very common reaction to tragedy. Though I do not believe in God or Heaven, I do have great faith in humankind: in our capacity to love and help each other, to share and give meaning to our joys and our sorrows. When I have felt most desolate, I have often asked 'Why me?'  Perhaps part of the answer lies in this book.

National Library of Australia Cataloguing-in-publication entry

Mortimer, Mary, 1944-

When your partner dies.

Bibliography.
ISBN 0 86806 417 3.
ISBN 0 86806 418 1 (pbk.)

1. Widowhood. 2. Bereavement. 3. Widows — Life skill guides.
4. Widowers — Life skill guides. I. Title

155.937 086 54

For *When your partner dies*, a technical examination provides this overview:

| | |
|---|---|
| • title | Provides a lot of information. This book is clearly about what happens when a partner dies |
| • subtitle | Not applicable |
| • author | Not helpful, since the author usually publishes in the field of librarianship |
| • foreword, preface, introduction | Preface explains content and author's intention |
| • publisher | Not helpful—this is a general publishing house for all types of material, not any one specialized area |
| • series | Not applicable |
| • contents and index | Contents confirm the subject of work, including practical nature |
| • text | Also confirms the subject |
| • cataloging-in-publication | Useful, though some headings are not in common use |

This book can be summarized as: 'A practical guide to dealing with the death of a partner'.

Key concepts include: coping with death, death of partners, guidance for dealing with bereavement, practical aspects of the aftermath of a death.

 ### ACTIVITY 2.2
*Practice analyzing material through the following activities:*

1. Choose a short (1-2 page) journal article. Using a timer, spend two minutes skiming and scanning the article. At the end of the time, write down the key concepts you identified, and summarize the article in one sentence. Then return and read the article entirely. How closely did your key concepts and summarization match the article? Repeat this activity with different articles, until you can arrive at the main topic/s of the articles simply by skimming and scanning.

2. Choose 2-3 resources from your library or personal collection. Use the technical examination process described above to determine the main topics of the resources. Which parts of the resources examined did you find most helpful for determining key topics and concepts?

# CHAPTER THREE
# Introduction to Library of Congress Subject Headings (LCSH)

## The LCSH Scheme

LCSH is an accumulation of subject headings established by the Library of Congress since 1898. The *List of subject headings for use in dictionary catalogs*, prepared by a committee of the American Library Association and published in 1895, was used as the basis for the Library's own list of subject headings.

The first edition of the Library of Congress list was printed in parts between 1909 and 1914. The title changed to *Library of Congress subject headings* with the eighth edition in 1975.

Headings are created as needed when works are cataloged for the collections of the Library of Congress. Headings are also retained in new editions of the list regardless of the recency or frequency of the list.

Inconsistencies in the formulation of headings can often be explained by the policies in force at the varying dates of their creation. LCSH is also an extremely large list, to which many catalogers and groups of catalogers contribute.

## Versions of LCSH

Library of Congress subject headings are available in the following formats:
- *Classification Web*—a fully searchable online interface for accessing up-to-date headings in *Library of Congress subject headings* (LCSH) and *Library of Congress genre/form terms for library and archival materials* (LCGFT). Classification Web also contains a number of other classification and subject headings databases, all updated daily. It is available by subscription at http://www.loc.gov/cds/classweb.
- *Library of Congress subject headings*—print version. The final printed edition of LCSH was the 35th, published in 2013. All later editions are issued annually as PDF files that may be freely downloaded from http://www.loc.gov/aba/cataloging/subject/.
- *Library of Congress authorities*—online at authorities.loc.gov. This version does not include headings combined with free-floating subdivisions, or instructions for use of geographic subdivisions.
- *Library of Congress linked data service*—a web service for browsing individual LCSH headings online at http://id.loc.gov/authorities/subjects.html. The Library of Congress Linked Data Service provides access to a range of standards and vocabularies, including LC *subject headings, LC genre/form terms, and LC children's subject headings.*

**Aids to using LCSH**
- *Subject headings manual*—an essential tool to be used in conjunction with LCSH. The manual contain Library of Congress policies and instructions on using LCSH, and provides lists of subdivisions that can be used with various topics. This ensures the cataloger uses headings and subdivisions correctly
  - The *Subject headings manual* is available online as part of a subscription to Cataloger's Desktop. It is also issued as a series of pdf files at http://www.loc.gov/aba/publications/FreeSHM/freeshmabout.html that can be freely downloaded
  - References to sections of the *Manual* are added to the headings throughout this workbook
- *LC subject headings approved lists*—an online monthly update of new and changed headings and subdivisions, available at http://www.loc.gov/aba/cataloging/subject/
- Other publications and additional information about LCSH can be found on the Cataloging and Acquisitions homepage http://www.loc.gov/aba/ within the Library of Congress website.


## Structure of LCSH

Library of Congress subject headings take the form of main topics with subdivisions, each element separated by a dash (e.g., **Atomic absorption spectroscopy—Instruments—Testing**)
- Main topics can be topical headings, form headings or name headings (see lists below)
- Subdivisions can be topical (e.g., objects, concepts or topics); form (e.g., juvenile literature); geographical; and/or chronological (e.g., period or historical subdivisions).

Notes and instructions within the entries provide information on:
- how to structure a heading
- which subdivisions can be used in conjunction with others
- the order in which subdivisions should be presented.

Notation in LCSH occurs as abbreviations within entries. Each entry lists:
- Main heading (preferred term)
- SN – Scope note
- UF – used for note (gives non-preferred synonyms for the main term)
- BT – broader topic
- RT – related topic
- SA – see also instructions indicating variations to the expected usage
- NT – narrower topic
- USE – refers one to the preferred term.

Scope notes are provided to ensure consistency of usage. A scope note:
- specifies the range of subject matter to which a heading should be applied

- draws necessary distinctions between related headings
- states which of several meanings is the one to use.

LCSH is a thesaurus, and is arranged in a standard thesaurus order, with entries in alphabetical order. However, because of the breadth of the topics in LCSH, some features of smaller, more specialized subject thesauri (e.g., hierarchical displays) are not included in LCSH. It is therefore important for catalogers to closely follow the notations and instructions, in order to ensure they are using the most appropriate subject heading.

## Types of Headings Found in LCSH

- **Topical** headings and subdivisions including:
    concepts
    types of objects
    disciplines
    methods and procedures
    activities
    industries
    classes of people
- **Form/Genre headings** for types of materials, e.g., dictionaries, biography etc.
- **Jurisdictional geographic names,** e.g., names of countries, states, provinces, etc.
- **Non-jurisdictional geographic names** including:
    geographic features
    areas and regions
    trails, parks and reserves
    city sections
    early cities, empires, kingdoms
- **Names of persons** incapable of authorship, including:
    groups of legendary, mythological and fictitious characters
    groups of gods
- Names of **families**, including:
    dynasties
    royal houses
- Names of **art works**
- Names of **chemicals, drugs and minerals**
- **Biological names**
- **Other proper names** including:
    languages
    computer languages and systems
    ethnic groups
    roads
    structures and buildings
    events
    trade names
    games

## Forms of Subject Headings (H 180)

Library of Congress subject headings may take several forms. Headings may be:

| single word | **Animals** |
|---|---|
| multiple words – direct order | **Animal populations** |
| multiple words – inverted order | **Animals, Mythical** |
| phrases – one concept | **Animal sounds** |
| phrases – two concepts | **Animals and history** |
| complex phrases | **Animals as aids for people with disabilities** |
| subdivided headings with topical components | **Animals—Abnormalities**<br>**Animals—Wintering**<br>**Animal welfare—Societies, etc.** |
| subdivided headings with place components | **Animals—Canada** |
| qualified terms | **Animal welfare (Jewish law)** |

Because LCSH was developed over a number of years using different formats at various times, there is no consistency within LCSH regarding which of the various types of headings are used. You must allow for the fact that any of these types may have been used. Do not just assume that a heading will be subdivided in a particular way.

## References (H 373)

LCSH contains cross-references that represent a mix of philosophies prevalent at different times in the history of the list. This explains why cross-referencing practices are not consistent within the list. Cross-references include:

- USE (or SEE) references
- broader and narrower term (hierarchical) relationships
- related term (associated) relationships
- general 'see also' relationships.

### USE (or SEE) references

USE references are made from unauthorized or **non-preferred** terms to an authorized or **preferred** heading. Under the preferred heading, the code UF precedes the headings not used.

For example,
**Cars (Automobiles)**
    USE   Automobiles
**Automobiles**
    UF    Cars (Automobiles)

**Automobiles** is the preferred term, and **Cars (Automobiles)** is the non-preferred term.

USE references are made from synonyms, variant spellings, variant forms of expression, alternate constructions of headings and older forms of headings. USE references may be employed even when the heading and unused words are not totally synonymous.

Older catalogs may use the word SEE instead of USE.

**References indicating hierarchical relationships (H 370)**
LCSH links subject headings in order to show the relationship between **broader (BT)** and **narrower (NT)** headings. This allows a user to make a search more general or more specific.

The hierarchical relationship is always reciprocal.
 For example,
**Exterior lighting**
    BT    Lighting
**Lighting**
    NT    Exterior lighting

A heading is linked only to the one immediately near it in the subject heading hierarchy (either immediately higher/broader or immediately lower/narrower). Catalogers wishing to view a complete hierarchy for a heading must trace it up or down the given links to see higher levels of more general terms or lower levels of more specific terms.

Three types of relationships are considered hierarchical:

*Genus/species relationships*
    **Apes**
        BT Primates

*Whole/part relationships*
    **Toes**
        BT Foot

*Instance (or generic topic/proper-named example) relationships*
    **Whitewater Lake (Wis.)**
        BT Lakes—Wisconsin
    [Whitewater Lake is an instance of a lake in Wisconsin]

**References indicating associated relationships**
LCSH also indicates relationships that are not broader or narrower but that are related.

 For example,
**Ornithology**
> RT    Birds

**Birds**
> RT    Ornithology

While there is no hierarchical relationship, terms are mentally associated to such an extent that the link reveals alternative headings that might be of interest.

**General references (H 371)**
A general reference is made not to a specific heading but to an entire group of headings, frequently listing one or more headings as an example. This occurs because it is impractical to list all possible headings.

 For example,
**Ethnic groups**
> SA *individual ethnic groups,* e.g., Hopi Indians

General references can be made from a generic heading to a group of headings beginning with the same word.

 For example,
**Chemistry**
> SA *headings beginning with the word*  Chemical

Sometimes general references lead to subdivisions. In these cases, the SA ('see also') notation is not a suggestion, but an instruction that the given subdivision must be used.

 For example, the reference:
**Economic history**
> SA *subdivision* Economic conditions *under names of countries, cities,* etc.

indicates that you must use the format *'<Country> - Economic conditions'* rather than the heading *'Economic history - <Country>'* for works about the economic history of countries or cities.

Sometimes general USE references can be made (H 374)

 For example,
**Access control**
> USE *subdivision* Access control *under types of archives, records, computers computer networks, and statistical and data-gathering services,* e.g. Computers—Access control; Psychiatric records—Access control

**EXERCISE 3.1**

*Use this extract from LCSH to answer the questions below:*

**Artisans** (May Subd Geog)
      UF     Artizans
                  Craftsmen
                  Craftspeople
                  Craftspersons
      BT     Skilled labor
      RT     Cottage industries
      NT     Apprentices
                  Diamond cutters
                  Glassworkers
                  Musical instrument makers
                  Women artisans

*What is the relationship between:*

1.  **Artisans** and **Craftsmen**

2.  **Artisans** and **Apprentices**

3.  **Artisans** and **Skilled labor**

4.  **Artisans** and **Cottage industries**

5.  Is **Craftsmen** an authorized / permitted term?

### EXERCISE 3.2

*Use LCSH to determine if these are acceptable headings. If not, write down the correct term.*

| Subject heading | Correct heading |
|---|---|
| 1.  Felix the Cat | |
| 2.  Guitar—Construction | |
| 3.  Fusion reactors—Fuels | |
| 4.  Fusion reactors—Germany | |
| 5.  Semi-conductors | |
| 6.  Guitar and harp music | |
| 7.  Heliophobus plants | |
| 8.  Seychelles—Coup d'etat, 1977 | |
| 9.  Coups d'etat—Seychelles | |
| 10. Tempo | |

## Arrangement of LCSH (print versions)

*Library of Congress subject headings* includes thousands of entries for headings, subdivisions, and references from non-preferred to preferred terms. Space is at a premium in the print volumes. To save space, therefore, there are no blank lines in the print versions of LCSH. Instead, typography and layout are used to separate entries.

Each printed page contains three columns, and every new entry (either a main heading or a non-preferred heading) is aligned to the left in its column. All the information below that heading is indented, including notations and subdivisions. A new heading reverts back to the far left of the column.

LCSH headings that are authorized for use as main subject entries are printed in bold type in the printed and pdf versions of LCSH. Authorized subdivisions are also printed in bold type. Subdivisions appear under the LCSH heading following a long dash, without repeating the heading. If two or more subdivisions are used, the main heading and the preceding subdivisions are replaced by additional long dashes:

**Libraries**
**—Public relations**    *(May Subd Geog)*
　　　UF    Public relations—Libraries *[Former heading]*
**— — Awards**    *(May Subd Geog)*
**— — — United States**
　　　NT    John Cotton Dana Library Public Relations Award

This heading would appear in a library catalog as:
**Libraries— Public relations— Awards— United States**

As noted earlier, the following symbols show the relationship between headings:
　　　UF    Used For
　　　BT    Broader Topic
　　　RT    Related Topic
　　　SA    See Also
　　　NT    Narrower Topic
　　　USE   Use

In addition, two abbreviated phrases are used to indicate geographic subdivision:
　　　*(May Subd Geog)*    Place names may follow the heading or subdivision.
　　　*(Not Subd Geog)*    The Library of Congress has decided not to subdivide by place.

Headings without either designation have not yet been considered for geographic subdivision. They may not currently be subdivided by place. As headings are constantly being reviewed, their status may change.

If the notation *(May Subd Geog)* appears a number of times in a subject heading sequence, insert the place name after the last subdivision containing the notation. (See **Geographic Subdivisions** in Chapter 7 for more details of the use of this notation.)

**EXERCISE 3.3**

*Study the following extract from LCSH, and answer the questions below:*

**Beverage industry**    *(May Subd Geog)*
　　　UF    Drink industry
　　　BT    Food industry and trade
　　　RT    Bottling
　　　NT    Alcoholic beverage industry
　　　　　 Bottled water industry
　　　　　 Brewing industry
　　　　　 Chicory beverage industry
　　　　　 Cider industry
　　　　　 Coffee industry

Distilling industries
Fruit drink industry
Mineral water industry
Non-alcoholic beverage industry
Soft drink industry
Tea trade
**— Employees**
**— — Labor unions**    *(May Subd Geog)*
**— Equipment and supplies**
NT    Beverage processing machinery
Beverage managers, Hotel
USE    Hotel beverage managers
**Beverage processing plants**    *(May Subd Geog)*
BT    Food processing plants
NT    Breweries
Distilleries
Milk plants
Wineries
**— Equipment and supplies**
NT    Beverage processing machinery


1.   *Write down all headings authorized for use as main subject entries, ignoring the subdivisions. Do not include broader and narrower terms.*




2.   *Write down all possible headings with subdivisions. Ignore geographic subdivisions.*




3.   *Using Canada as the place name, write down all possible headings with geographic subdivisions.*

**Filing order in LCSH print versions**

Headings are filled alphabetically although in the print and online 'search' versions:

- the dash (–) and the comma (,) file before letters, in that order, and
- in the print version, geographic subdivisions file at the end of a sequence.

The examples of forms of headings listed earlier in this chapter would file in the following order in the print version:

| LCSH terminology | Type of heading |
|---|---|
| **Animal populations** | direct heading |
| **Animal products as feed** | phrase heading |
| **Animal welfare** | direct heading |
| **Animal welfare—Societies, etc** | subdivided heading |
| **Animal welfare (Jewish law)** | qualified heading |
| **Animals** | single word heading |
| **Animals—Abnormalities** | heading with subdivision |
| **Animals—Wintering** | heading with subdivision |
| **Animals, Mythical** | indirect heading |
| **Animals and history** | phrase |

It is particularly important to be aware of LCSH's filing practices when using the print version of the scheme. Headings like 'Animal/ Animals', with all their subdivisions, can span a number of pages in the scheme. Knowing how headings are filed will ensure you don't overlook a relevant heading.

# CHAPTER FOUR
# Using Classification Web (LCSH Online)

### What is *Classification Web*

*Classification Web* is the web-based version of the LC classification scheme (LCC) and of a suite of subject heading schemes, including the LC subject heading scheme (LCSH), LC name headings, juvenile subject headings, and genre/form headings.

While a major focus of the product is the Library of Congress Classification, *Classification Web* also provides online access to LCSH. *Classification Web* is used to search, display and navigate the *Library of Congress subject headings* (LCSH) data using a standard Web browser. One can also correlate a LCSH heading with its corresponding DDC number, and with LCC numbers.

*Classification Web* is a no-frills product, designed to allow you to specifically search for class numbers and subject headings. Ancillary tools which provide guidance on the use of LCSH, like the *Subject headings manual*, are not included. The *Subject headings manual* and other documents of value for subject cataloging are available as part of a separate subscription to a different Library of Congress online product, *Cataloger's Desktop*.

LCSH via *Classification Web* allows catalogers to search the LCSH database in a number of ways:
- using 'Search' to find headings or subdivisions
- using 'Browse' to find headings or subdivisions
- using keywords to find headings or subdivisions
- viewing a subject authority record for a LCSH heading
- finding Library of Congress Classification numbers that correlate to LC Subject headings
- finding LC Subject headings that correlate to LCC numbers
- finding Dewey Decimal Classification numbers that correlate to LC Subject headings
- finding LC Subject headings that correlate to DDC numbers

### Accessing Classification Web

Access to *Classification Web* is by subscription, at http://classificationweb.net. The Main Menu allows you to access each 'product' database separately. The various products are not connected—each is entered and searched separately—although there are provisions within the *Search LC subject headings* product to correlate subject headings with classifications.

## Finding Your Way around *Classification Web*

The various subject heading products (*LCSH*, *LC Name Headings*, *Sears Juvenile Headings*, *Medium of Performance* and *Genre/Form Headings*) have similar 'Subject Search' screens, which are all used in the same manner.

Although the 'Subject Search' and 'Subject Browse' screens looks fairly sparse, there are provisions for searching by subject heading, keyword, classification number, and for free-floating subdivisions. *Classification Web* supports:
- truncation searching (input a partial search term; there are no truncation symbols)
- boolean (i.e., AND, OR and NOT) operations
- mathematical (i.e., less than, greater than, etc.) operations
- wild-card characters (? matches any single character; * matches multiple characters)
- phrase and proximity searches
- all words in a term – there are no stopwords; 'and', 'of' 'the' etc. within headings are searchable.

The advanced options for the 'Subject Search' screen are at the bottom of the screen, using the *Search tips and options* link. When opened, this area provides basic instructions on how to use the search screen, as well as display and search options. The options chosen will remain for the duration of your session and revert to the default options when you log out.

 *Always open the* Search tips and options *link and ensure the settings you want are nominated.*

### Browse vs Query

There are two methods of searching: browsing, and query searches. The results display different information.

**'Browse'** searches the index of the LCSH database, and finds all occurrences of a term that begin with the subject heading nominated. Browse searches cannot use Boolean operators, but you can navigate up and down the resulting index list. Browse searches return full LCSH entries including all broader, narrower, related and non-preferred terms.

A **'Query'** is run through the **'Search'** screen and displays records that match your search terms, whether your term starts the subject heading string or is included within the heading. Search queries can be constructed using Boolean operators and wild cards. Search basic queries and Boolean queries return reduced entries containing only broader, related and non-preferred terms but not narrower terms.

A single word search, whether in the 'Browse' screen or the 'Search' screen, will automatically default to an index search (i.e., a 'Browse' search). However, if using the Search page, you can change the '*Search tips and options*' to run a basic query or a Boolean query instead of the default 'browse'.

Although a **query** matches your search terms exactly, and therefore returns more relevant subject headings, you may miss seeing similar headings that would be evident using a 'browse' search. For example, a query search for 'female athletes' will return the full record for the heading 'Women athletes', which is the preferred term. However, it does not alert you to a range of other headings that may also be useful, including 'Women athletes—Physiology', Women athletes in literature', 'Women athletic trainers', etc., which are displayed when using the 'Browse' search.

 *Always check your* Search tips and options *settings when using the Search screen to ensure you have ticked the type of search you wish to run.*

 **ACTIVITY 4.1**
*Use the 'Search LC Subject Headings' database from the Classification Web main menu. Run a query (set your search options to 'Run a basic query' on the 'Search' screen) to find the following headings. Note the information provided.*

1. Holiday decorations

2. Swindlers and swindling

3. Animal attacks

4. Motor ability in children

5. Swim clubs

*Now find the same headings using 'Browse' (either change your search options to 'Run browse' or return to the main menu and choose 'Browse LC Subject Headings' – both will produce the same results). Note the different information received.*

*Discuss the benefits and drawbacks of each option. Which do you prefer for the work you do?*

**Structured vs Unstructured order**
If you are searching for subject headings that include subdivisions, results of a search can display differently, depending on whether you query using structured (double dashes between subdivisions) or unstructured (no dashes between subdivisions) search options.

***Structured*** heading or subdivision searches will display the results in a hierarchical order. Structured displays show a heading's first alphabetical subdivision and all that subdivision's sub-subdivisions and references, before listing the next subdivision and its sub-subdivisions. This is similar to the order seen in the print version of LCSH.

 Small business—Law and legislation
Small business investment companies

Note that if using structured searches, double dashes must be included to indicate the subdivision component of a heading.

*Unstructured* heading searches display their results in dictionary order, interfiling a subject, its subdivisions and references with other subjects and subdivisions. Unstructured searches do not require any punctuation in the search query. You can run an unstructured search by ticking the *'search for subject headings without requiring double dashes between subdivisions'* box under 'Search Options'.

 Small business investment companies
Small business—Law and legislation

Further details about choosing query and display options for LCSH online are available in the 'help' screens of *Classification Web*.

### Keyword searches

If a cataloger knows the exact terminology used in a subject heading, this can be input into the Search 'subject heading' box for quick and efficient searching. However, in cases where you are not aware of the exact LC heading it is better to use the Search 'keyword' box. Inputting one or more words into the 'keyword' box will run a query to locate all records that contain those words. All keyword searches support phrase and proximity searches, and will return subdivision results without requiring double dashes between a heading and a subdivision. This provides more flexibility to the cataloger for finding terms.

 *Even when you are fairly sure of your subject heading, it is a good idea to use the 'keyword' search box to ensure you pick up all variations of your term.*

### Free-floating subdivisions

Classification Web has provision for searching and browsing free-floating subdivisions, in structured or unstructured order. This is useful to establish the correct format for a free-floating subdivision, and to see the scope notes attached to its use. However, there are limitations to the use of this field. It is intended only as a search of the list of free-floating subdivisions, not as a way of finding subject headings with free-floating subdivisions attached. Because of this, **if you input a term in the subject heading field and a term in the free-floating subdivision field, only the subject heading field will be searched**. In other words, only one search field box can be used per search. (Note that you can combine subject terms and subdivisions on the same line using one of the 'subject heading' boxes, but not in the free-floating subdivision boxes.)

## Reading the Results Screens

Depending on the searching options chosen, different amounts of information will be displayed, in different filing order. However, all result displays will include the following information:

- Hyperlinked Broader, Related and (sometimes) Narrower Terms, which will take you to the relevant main entries for those terms
- Hyperlinked LC Classification numbers
- Additional links, in a drop-down white button after the entry, to:
  - the subject authority record in MARC format
  - a LC subject/DDC correlation search
  - a LC subject / LC classification correlation search
  - the heading in LC structured (i.e., 'browse') filing order.

## LCSH Classification Correlations

*Classification Web* provides the ability to view the Library of Congress Classification (LCC) or Dewey Decimal Classification (DDC) numbers most frequently used with a specific LC subject heading or subject heading string. This can be done by clicking the option box next to a subject heading from the LC Search Results page, and choosing '*Dewey correlation*' or '*LC class correlation*'. This brings you into the 'Bibliographic Correlations' database of *Classification Web*. The resulting Correlations Search screen indicates your original search text and search type (LCSH to DDC, or LCSH to LCC), followed by a list of classification numbers and the number of times they have been applied to your subject term.

More, and different, correlations can be performed by choosing different options from the drop-down 'Search type' menu, including options for correlating a classification number to a LCSH heading. This is a good way to search for appropriate LC subject headings if you have a DDC number or a LCC number.

Remember that LCSH also includes hyperlinks to recommended LC classification numbers as part of a heading's main entry. The correlation feature provides classification numbers for those topics that do not have a recommended LCC number, and/or alternative LCC numbers for those with recommended LCC numbers.

Note that the correlation feature only provides a rough correlation of terms to class numbers, based on frequency of use in the Library of Congress catalog. Library of Congress cataloging mainly uses LC classification, not Dewey, so the number of DDC class numbers that correlate to a subject heading may be relatively small and therefore sometimes not totally accurate. Correlation is a useful starting point for developing a DDC class number or for confirming your use of a particular number. However, **it should not be used as a substitute for devising LCC or DDC numbers, and all numbers used should be checked** both for accuracy and for relevance to the item in hand.

### EXERCISE 4.2

*Use the 'Search LC Subject Headings' and 'Bibliographic Correlations' databases for the following tasks:*

*Locate the following subject headings in Classification Web, and find LCC and DDC correlations for them. Note that you may have more than one classification number for your results:*

1. Dogs—Judging        LCC: _____

                       DDC: _____


2. Politics and culture    LCC: _____

                       DDC: _____


3. Rice                LCC: _____

                       DDC: _____


*Using the Bibliographic Correlation database, find a subject heading for the following LCC numbers:*

4. BL290              _____

5. UG734.A98          _____

6. PS3511.A9327       _____


*Using the Bibliographic Correlation database, find a subject heading for the following DDC numbers:*

7. 599.539            _____

8. 647.944            _____

9. 636.8089100222     _____

## Filing Order in *Classification Web*

In *Classification Web*, there are some filing differences when viewing displays, based on your search strategy and how punctuation is filed. For structured 'Browse' and 'Search' searches, dashes are filed before letters (as in the print version), but commas are ignored.

 A typical filing sequence would read:
Animals—Poetry
Animals and history
Animals, Mythical

For unstructured Basic Queries or Boolean Queries, results are not returned in any particular order, although they tend to be in LC record number order. This means you should scroll through the entire result set to ensure you see all relevant subject headings.

 A Basic Query search for the term 'animals' retrieved 204 results, including the above three in this order:
Animals, Mythical (4th in list)
Animals and history (84th in list, after headings like 'Zoology, Economic')
Animals—Poetry (169th in list)

## Putting it All Together

Classification Web offers a quick and easy way to search Library of Congress subject headings, and provides value adding via links to authority records and classification numbers. It has a number of search options, some of which present their results in very different formats to that of the printed product. Catalogers can determine the best options for their needs and for the way they work. The exercise below is designed to provide practice in searching LCSH online, using all the features of *Classification Web*.

Regardless of which format of LCSH you use—print, pdf or online—you will be interrogating the same database of headings, so your results will contain the same subject terms. However, not every subject term will be useful to assign as a subject heading. How to assign headings is the focus of our next chapter.

## EXERCISE 4.3

*Using Classification Web, find subject headings, with subdivisions as appropriate, for the following topics:*

| Topic | Subject heading |
|---|---|
| 1. Cooking with rice | _____ |
| 2. Rock lobsters | _____ |
| 3. Conflicts of interest | _____ |
| 4. Low sodium diet | _____ |
| 5. Stained glass | _____ |
| 6. Supervision of spiritual directors | _____ |
| 7. Tibetan gilt bronzes | _____ |
| 8. Women heroes on television | _____ |
| 9. Toybraries | _____ |
| 10. Carbon content of plant biomass | _____ |

# CHAPTER FIVE
# Assigning LC Subject Headings (H 180)

## Introduction
Understanding the arrangement and structure of LCSH, whether in print or online form, is useful when you begin to search the list for appropriate subject headings to assign. Since LCSH is a pre-coordinated list (that is, the headings have already been assembled in a specific order), you must 'match' your concepts to both the words, and the order, used by LCSH. This chapter will outline some practical tips for finding headings, as well as LCSH's set of formal guidelines for assigning headings.

## Finding Subject Headings in LCSH
If a subject has various aspects, you must decide which is the main aspect and which are sub-topics. Start with what you feel is the most important aspect, and find its heading in LCSH. Are the other aspects covered as subdivisions of that main heading? Is it possible to tie the various aspects together? If so, accept that heading. If not, start at a different aspect and look in LCSH. Can you tie them together now?

 ***Tip 1.*** *Accept the heading that ties all the aspects together.*

The heading that ties all aspects together may not always be obvious – LCSH's interpretation may not be the same as yours! For example, look at these items from Exercise 7.1 in this workbook:
- The subject for 'Extensions to buildings' is fairly obvious: **buildings** as the main subject and **extensions** as the sub-topic
- But with John Brown's raid on Harpers Ferry it is not so obvious where to start. If you start with the raid, you will not be able to tie in Harpers Ferry. Try **Harpers Ferry** and see if you can use the raid as a subdivision.

If you can't fit all aspects in one heading, you may need to use two headings. But try to fit all aspects together first.

 ***Tip 2:*** *Always check LCSH.*

Don't assume you know a heading, even if you've used it in the past. You may find a more appropriate narrower term or related term listed under the heading you were planning to use. Or you may find that you didn't transcribe the correct form of the heading, or didn't spell it correctly – or the heading may have changed! It is good practice to always confirm your heading in LCSH.

**Tip 3:** *Keep looking.*

Always look at the LCSH entries appearing before and after the heading you plan to use. There may be other types of headings that begin with the same root term as your topic, or the physical arrangement of LCSH may place the heading further from the sequence you check than you expect.

 For example, if looking for a heading for the topic 'mythical animals' some possibilities are:

- **Animal mythology**
- **Animals—Mythical**
- **Animals—Mythology**
- **Animals, Mythical**

The *last* one is correct. But if you were using the print version of LCSH, or the display from the online 'search' option, you would have to search to the end of the 'animal/animals' sequence to find the correct heading.

 **Tip 4:** *Try different aspects as the main heading until you can find a satisfactory combination.*

If you can't find an appropriate combination for your complex topic under one aspect, always try to look under another aspect as the heading. In the 'animal mythology' example above, if no heading was available when you finished looking at all the 'animal' headings then you should go to 'mythology' and look at all possible heading there.

## Guidelines for Assigning Headings

Once you have analyzed the item and decided what topics are the subject of the work, you must determine which of these are to be included as headings. LCSH provides guidelines in the *Subject headings manual*, section H180:

### General rule
Assign one or more subject headings that best summarize the overall contents of the work. The aim is to provide access to the most important topics.

### Number of headings
This will vary with the work being cataloged. Generally, a maximum of six headings is appropriate. If more than one heading is used, arrange the headings in order of their predominance in the work.

### Order of headings
- Assign the heading that represents the predominant topic of the work as the first subject heading.

- If a work has two equally important major topics, assign them one after the other, before any headings for secondary topics.
- Assign headings for secondary topics in any order following the headings for the major topics.

## Specificity

Assign the most specific heading that represents the contents of the work. Where a specific heading is not possible, assign a heading that is broader or more general than the topic.

 For example,

**Mathematics** and **Trigonometry** are not normally assigned to the same work.

## Works on a single topic

Assign the one heading that exactly represents the contents of the work.

 For example,

| | |
|---|---|
| *Title* | The world within the tide pool |
| *Subject heading* | **Tide pool ecology** |

## Subtopic not normally subsumed under a heading

Normally a work on a single topic can be expected to cover a range of subtopics. If, within such a work, there is a subtopic that falls outside the scope of the expected range, allocate headings for the main topic plus an additional heading for the subtopic. The subtopic should cover at least 20% of the work to warrant a separate heading.

 For example,

| | |
|---|---|
| *Title* | Statistical planning for agricultural operations in Godavari |
| *Subject headings* | **1. Agriculture—India—Godavari—Statistics** |
| | **2. Rice—India—Godavari** |

## Multi-topic works

For works on more than one topic treated separately, assign headings to bring out each concept individually.

 For example,

| | |
|---|---|
| *Title* | Bibliography on snow, ice and frozen ground |
| *Subject headings* | **1. Snow—Bibliography** |
| | **2. Ice—Bibliography** |
| | **3. Frozen ground—Bibliography** |

## Hierarchical considerations

Special guidelines apply for related topics that fit under a common theme within a work.

### a) Two or three related topics in a work

If a heading exists that represents precisely the two or three topics, assign it and not the two or three headings.

 For example,

| | |
|---|---|
| *Title* | The distinctive excellences of Greek and Latin |
| *Subject heading* | **1. Classical literature** |

(Separate headings are not used because Classical literature includes both Greek and Latin and nothing else)

**b) Rule of three**

If a broad heading exists, but includes more than the two or three topics in question, assign the two or three headings, not the broader heading.

 For example,

| | |
|---|---|
| *Title* | Travels in Brazil, Ecuador and Peru |
| *Subject headings* | **1. Brazil—Description and travel** |
| | **2. Ecuador—Description and travel** |
| | **3. Peru—Description and travel** |
| | (not the more inclusive South America) |

**c) Rule of four (four or more related topics in a work)**

Do not assign a separate heading for each topic where a single heading that covers all topics can be used.

If no such heading exists, assign separate headings for up to four topics. If there are more than four topics, assign several very comprehensive headings or a single form heading.

 For example,

**Automobiles, Racing** (For a work on hot rods, go-karts, dragsters, sprint cars and Formula One cars.)

**Multi-element works**

If a work treats a single subject from different aspects or contains various elements of one topic, use one pre-coordinated heading, if there is one available.

 For example,

| | |
|---|---|
| *Title* | Chemical plant management in the U.S.A. |
| *Subject heading* | **1. Chemical plants—United States—Management** |

However there are many subjects that are much more complex with no pre-coordinated heading available for use. In such cases, assign headings for each concept individually.

 For example,

| | |
|---|---|
| *Title* | A method of setting up the eigenvalue problem for the linear, shallow-water wave equation for irregular bodies of water with variable water depth and application to bays and harbors in Hawai'i. |
| *Subject headings* | **1. Ocean waves** |
| | **2. Eigenvalues** |
| | **3. Oceanography—Data processing** |
| | **4. Bays—Hawaii** |
| | **5. Harbors—Hawaii** |

**Principle versus a specific case**

If a work discusses a principle and illustrates the principle by referring to a specific case, assign a heading for the principle and also a heading for the specific case, if appropriate.

 For example, a work on the anatomy of vertebrates that illustrates this by reference to cats would get two subject headings, one for the main topic and one for the example.

| | |
|---|---|
| *Title* | The anatomy of vertebrates |
| *Subject headings* | **1. Vertebrates—Anatomy** |
| | **2. Cats—Anatomy** |

**Viewpoint of author or publisher**

Always consider this and assign a heading if useful.

 For example,

If the work is written primarily for a juvenile audience use the subdivision

**—Juvenile literature**

If a general textbook is intended for specific persons, allocate a heading for the topic and one for the special interest or application.

 For example,

| | |
|---|---|
| *Title* | Psychology for nurses |
| *Subject headings* | **1. Psychology** |
| | **2. Nursing—Psychological aspects** |

**Concepts in titles**

Titles and subtitles are important because they sometimes state in the words of the author or publisher the subject matter of the work. Assign headings for each topic so identified if it is discussed in the work.

 For example,

| | |
|---|---|
| *Title* | Easy-to-make wooden candlesticks, chandeliers and lamps |
| *Subject headings* | **1. Woodwork** |
| | **2. Candlesticks** |
| | **3. Chandeliers** |
| | **4. Lamps** |

## EXERCISE 5.1

*Using LCSH, provide a subject heading that best represents the following topics:*

| Topic | Subject heading |
|---|---|
| 1. The sea | |
| 2. Adoption services | |
| 3. Adriatic Islands | |
| 4. Children as actors | |
| 5. Ways to monitor fetal heart rate | |
| 6. The impact of highway traffic noise | |
| 7. Oceanic drilling ships in the Atlantic | |
| 8. Catalan political satire | |
| 9. Introduction to prehistoric agriculture | |
| 10. The wonders of horseradish | |

### General guidelines—additional aspects
#### a) Place
If a work involves a specific geographic area, indicate the area by a subject heading or a subdivision.

#### b) Time
Express the chronological aspects significant to the contents of the work in situations where the Library of Congress subject heading system allows it.

#### c) Named entities
Assign headings from the name authority file or subject authority file for individual persons, families, corporate bodies, projects etc. that are significant to the content of the work.

#### d) Form
Assign form headings and subdivisions to represent what the item itself is—that is, its format or the particular type or arrangement of data that it contains—in situations where headings or subdivisions for these types of materials exist.

**Form subject headings**

Form refers to the manner or style in which material is presented, i.e., the particular character or method of presentation of information (e.g., Aerial photographs, Biography, Catalogs and collections, Dictionaries, Encyclopedias, Musical settings, Programmed instruction).

Form can be designated by
- a topical subject heading with form subdivision
  or
- a form subject heading as a main heading.

Assign form subject headings as main headings to:
- works that discuss the form of the material as their main topic

 For example,
  **Blogs** (for works that are *about* blogs)
    use the subdivision **—Blogs** for works that *are* blogs

- works produced in a particular format for users with disabilities

 For example,
  **Large type books** (often used for fiction in large print)
  **Talking books** (works reproduced on tape, disc or record for the visually impaired)

- rare books. If a work is held for its quality, uniqueness, or particular characteristics as a physical entity, a form subject to highlight this can be used

 For example,
  **Book ornamentation**
  **Bookbinding**
  **Chapbooks**
  **Early printed books**
  **Fine books**
  **Small press books**

**If a subject heading is the same as another access point (H184)**

Subject headings fulfil a different role from other access points—author, title, corporate body and so on. Therefore, name subject headings should always be assigned to reflect the subject being discussed, even if the name is also used as a title or author access point.

 For example,
  *Title*            The operation of the American Red Cross: an official viewpoint
  *Author entry*   **I. American Red Cross**
  *Subject heading*  **1. American Red Cross**

**EXERCISE 5.2**

*Using LCSH, provide a subject heading that best represents the following topics. In some instances, the answer may require more than one heading:*

| Topic | Subject heading |
|---|---|
| 1.  Morris West's slide collections | |
| 2.  Water conservation and irrigation efficiency | |
| 3.  Cartoon-makers | |
| 4.  Electric condensers | |
| 5.  Music for organ and flute | |
| 6.  Sulky racing | |
| 7.  Harmony on the keyboard | |
| 8.  Prehistoric cartography | |
| 9.  The benefits of asparaginic acid | |
| 10. Bakery products | |

    Points to remember about assigning LCSH subject headings:

1.  Make sure your heading is exactly as it appears in LCSH.
2.  This extends to American spelling e.g., **Aging**, or **Fetal heart rate.**
3.  Qualifiers are included e.g., **Felix the Cat (Fictitious character).**
4.  Punctuation is important e.g,. Semi-conductors is wrong, **Semiconductors** is correct.
5.  Capitalisation is important, e.g., **Agriculture, Prehistoric.**
6.  Be careful to follow the subdivisions in a heading.
7.  Make sure you look down all the subdivisions—some geographic subdivisions are handled as special cases.
8.  Look at the scope notes and SA references e.g., **Coups** in general are assigned quite different headings to a specific coup. The notes and references will guide you to the correct heading.
9.  Never assume that because one heading is formed in a certain way, similar concepts will be the same e.g., **Guitar and harp music** vs **Guitars (2) with jazz ensemble.**
10. Don't subdivide geographically unless you are told to—a blank means 'NO'.

# CHAPTER SIX
# MARC

## Coding Subject Headings

Subject headings are coded into the 6xx fields of MARC. The fields used with Library of Congress subject headings are given below. Tags 653-69x are designed for coding specialist thesaurus terms or terms from faceted subject schemes, and are not discussed in this book.

| Tag | Field | Purpose |
|-----|-------|---------|
| 600 | Personal Name | This field is used for resources where a person is the subject, such as a biography. The author of a work will go into a 100 or 700 field |
| 610 | Corporate Name | This field is used for resources where an organization is the topic being discussed. Corporate bodies that are authors of a work go into 110 or 710 fields |
| 611 | Meeting Name | This field is used for resources about a conference or meeting, not for the conference proceedings. For conference proceedings, the conference name goes into a 111 or 711 field |
| 630 | Uniform Title | This field is used when a resource that is the subject of a work has a uniform title, e.g., 'Bible' |
| 648 | Chronological Term | This field is used when the subject of the work is a chronological term—e.g., a date. More commonly, time periods are indicated as chronological subdivisions, using the subfield code $y |
| 650 | Topical Term | This field is for the topic of the resource. Use the authorized form of the subject, taken from LCSH |
| 651 | Geographic Name | This field is used when a resource is about a place. Use the authorized form of the place name, taken from LCSH or an authority file |
| 655 | Genre/Form | This term is used to indicate the style (genre, e.g., horror fiction) of a resource, or its format (form, e.g., map) |

All the 6xx fields are repeatable. The most commonly used tags are 650 and 651, then 600.

Subfield indicators and subfield codes are used with 6xx fields. The second indicator specifies the source of the subject heading. Library of Congress subject headings are identified by "0" as the second indicator.

Subfield codes are added directly after the main heading, without spacing. The dash (—) that precedes a subdivision is not recorded in the MARC record.

All 6xx fields end with a mark of punctuation (.), a closing parenthesis, or an open date entry (e.g., '$y1993- '). If the final subfields are $2, $3 or $4 (subfields which provide codes indicating controlled vocabularies used), the mark of punctuation precedes those subfields.

## Subject Subdivisions

MARC caters for LCSH's use of subdivisions by special subfields. They are normally added to the main heading in the following order:

$x    General subdivision (for most topical subdivisions)
$y    Chronological subdivision (e.g.,  —18th century)
$z    Geographic subdivision (e.g.,  —Africa)
$v    Form subdivision (e.g.,  —Periodicals)

The form subdivision ($v) is usually placed at the end of the subject heading string.

However, the *Subject headings manual* (H 1075, 1d) says: "Code a form subdivision as an $x subfield when it represents a form that the item is *about*. This often occurs when a subdivision that is normally a form subdivision is followed by another form subdivision."

 For example,
**Canada$vMaps**  (for actual maps of Canada)
*but*
**Canada$xMaps$vBibliography**  (for a bibliography of maps of Canada)

## Genre/Form Headings

Catalogers can indicate a genre or form of material (eg 'Horror films') by using a special list of Genre/Form headings available from the Library of Congress. These are coded as 655 entries, with the second indicator '7' and a subfield code $2lcgft (to indicate the term was taken from the controlled vocabulary of LC genre/form terms rather than from LCSH).

Genre/Form headings stand alone as additional headings, and may not be subdivided. They take the form:
**655 #7 $a**[*genre term*]**$2**[*source code*]
 For example,
**655 #7$aHorror films$2lcgft**

Changes to MARC coding have been implemented which allow Genre/Form headings to be more readily identified via changes to the 008 and 040 field in authority records, and via changes to the indicators and subfield codes in bibliographic records. Refer to LCSH *Frequently Asked Questions about Library of Congress Genre/Form terms for Library and Archival Materials (LCGFT)* http://www.loc.gov/catdir/cpso/genre_form_faq.pdf for more information and updates on this topic. In addition, in January 2016 the Library of Congress published a draft *Genre/Form Terms Manual*, with guidelines and instructions for assigning these terms, available at http://www.loc.gov/aba/publications/FreeLCGFT/freelcgft.html.

## MARC Coding Examples

The *MARC 21 concise format for bibliographic data* is freely available on the Internet at www.loc.gov/marc/. Here are some examples of how to use MARC to code subjects.

### Name subject headings 600, 610, 611
*Model*
600  _0  $aPersonal name$xsubject subdivision.
610  _0  $aCorporate name$xsubject subdivision.
611  _0  $aConference name$xsubject subdivision.

600    10 $aDepardieu, Gerard,$d1948–
600    10 $aChristie, Agatha,$d1890-1976$vHandbooks, manuals, etc.
610    20 $aRutgers University$xHistory.
610    20 $aNASA Advisory Council.$bSolar System Exploration Committee.
611    10 $aSymposium on Carcinogenesis, Mechanisms of Action,$cLondon,$d1959.
611    20 $aCongress$d(1814-1815 :$cVienna)

### Uniform title subject heading 630
*Model*
630  _0  $aUniform title$xsubject subdivision.

630    00 $aMicrosoft Excel (Computer file)
630    00 $aLinux$vPeriodicals.
630    00 $aBible$xInfluence$xSlavic civilization.
630    00 $aLos Angeles times$vIndexes$vPeriodicals.

### Topical subject heading 650
*Model*
650  _0  $aTopical subject$xsubject subdivision$zgeographic subdivision$ychronological subdivision$vform subdivision.

The order of elements in topical subject headings usually follows the order shown above. It will sometimes vary depending on how the subjects are authorized to be subdivided. This is particularly so for geographic subdivisions that follow the last subject heading or subdivision that can be subdivided geographically.

Note that subjects can have geographic subdivisions in 650 subfield $z if there is a place aspect to a topic.

650    _0 $aReal estate business$xTechnological innovations$zUnited States.

650    _0 $aInternet marketing$zUnited States.

650    _0 $aMacadamia nut industry$zHawaii$xHistory.

650    _0 $aAuthors, American$y20th century$vBiography.

650    _0 $aDetective and mystery stories, English$xStories, plots, etc.$vHandbooks, manuals, etc.

650    _0 $aTechnology$xSocial aspects$vCongresses.

650    _0 $aNumismatics$xCollectors and collecting.

650    _0 $aArchives$zUnited States$vDirectories.

650    _0 $aJapanese Americans$zCalifornia$vNewspapers.

## Geographic subject heading 651

*Model*

651  _0  $aGeographic subject heading$xsubject subdivision$ychronological subdivision$vform subdivision.

651    _0 $aDenver (Colo.)$vNewspapers.

651    _0 $aLos Angeles (Calif.)

651    _0 $aColorado$xDescription and travel.

651    _0 $aRocky Mountains.

651    _0 $aNile River.

651    _0 $aAlaska$xBoundaries$zCanada.

651    _0 $aSpeedway (Ind.)$xMaps.

651    _0 $aUnited States$xPolitics and government$y1853-1857.

A more complete discussion of MARC coding is available in the 'Learn Library Skills Series' publication, *Cataloging the RDA Way* by L Farkas and H Rowe.

 **EXERCISES**

*Practice MARC coding by adding MARC tags, indicators and subfield codes to your exercise answers (where applicable) in the following chapters.*

# CHAPTER SEVEN
# Subdivisions

## Introduction

Subdivisions are used extensively in LCSH. They allow a number of different concepts to be combined in a single subject heading. Subdivisions serve two functions in LCSH:

- they make a subject more specific
- they sub-arrange a large number of items under one heading in a catalog.

Some subdivisions are given in LCSH but these represent only a small fraction of possible combinations of headings and subdivisions. Others may be applied as instructed in the *Library of Congress subject headings manual*.

Authority to use subdivisions with a particular heading can be found in four places:

1. under the subject heading entry in LCSH
2. as a SA note under the general subject heading that represents the topic you want
3. in the list of Free-Floating Subdivisions (this does not imply uncontrolled use)
4. as a Pattern Heading.

## Types of Subdivisions

There are four types of subdivisions: **topical, form, chronological** and **geographic**. Detailed instructions for assigning them appear in various sections of the *Subject headings manual*.

### Topical subdivisions

These are used to limit the concept expressed by the heading to a special subtopic.

 **Corn—Harvesting**
**Automobiles—Motors—Carburetors**

### Form subdivisions

These indicate the form in which the material on a subject is organized and presented. They are usually added as the last element in the string of terms. Form subdivisions can generally be used with any topic and are therefore not usually listed as subdivisions under every heading. Most form subdivisions are indicated by a general *see also* reference under the heading representing the form as a whole.

 **Newspapers**
SA *subdivision* Newspapers *under subjects*.

Detailed guidance on the use of form subdivisions is given in the *Subject headings manual* at section H 1075.

**EXERCISE 7.1**

*Using LCSH, allocate suitable subject headings to the following. Include one or more subdivisions to make your heading more specific.*

| Topic | Subject heading |
|---|---|
| 1. The cost of constructing railroads | |
| 2. Extensions to buildings | |
| 3. Synthesis in organic chemistry | |
| 4. Data processing in credit bureaus | |
| 5. The rights and wages of employees in credit unions | |
| 6. John Brown's raid on Harpers Ferry | |
| 7. The 1929 depression in Chicago | |
| 8. The diagnosis of unipolar depression | |
| 9. Renaissance engraving | |
| 10. Hunting with bows and arrows | |

**Chronological or period subdivisions**

These are used to limit a heading to a particular time period. These subdivisions may:

- denote chronological sequences under countries

  *eg* **Great Britain—History—George VI, 1936-1952**

- mark significant dates in the evolution of a subject

  *eg* **Philosophy, French—18th century**

  **Christian life—History—Middle Ages, 600-1500**

- reflect the history of a particular subject. In these cases, the periods used will not be relevant to other subjects, and so will not be consistent throughout LCSH

  *eg* **American literature—1783-1850**

Subdivisions on the history of a particular subject are filed chronologically before the alphabetical list of topical headings in print versions of LCSH:

**Christian art and symbolism**
   **—To 500**
   **—Medieval, 500-1500**
   **—Renaissance, 1450-1600**
   **—Modern period, 1500-**
   —(*And then topical headings alphabetically*)

*Applying period subdivisions*
Use a maximum of two subdivisions to denote chronological periods with any subject heading. If the work in hand covers more than two chronological periods then use the heading without period subdivisions.

 For example, an item on Christian art and symbolism from 100AD to 1600 covers more than two of the available periods, so would be assigned only the heading:
   **Christian art and symbolism**

If the work in hand falls partly in and partly out of one period, either use two periods, or none. Do not use only one period if material in the work also falls outside that period.

 For example, an item on Christian art and symbolism from 400AD to 1200 should be assigned:
   **Christian art and symbolism—To 500**
   **Christian art and symbolism— Medieval, 500-1500**
   or just:
   **Christian art and symbolism.**

**Geographic subdivisions (H 830)**
These may be added when the designation *(May Subd Geog)* appears after a heading or subdivision. The designation *(Not Subd Geog)* after a heading or subdivision indicates that the Library of Congress has made a decision not to subdivide by place. Headings without either designation may currently not be subdivided by place because they have yet to be reviewed to determine whether a geographic subdivision is possible or desirable.

If a heading contains both a geographic subdivision and a topical or form subdivision, the location of the geographic subdivision depends on which elements can be divided by place. If a geographic subdivision is allowable in two or more places in the sequence, position the place name after the last subdivision that allows you to subdivide geographically.

 *Chapter Nine of this book contains further information about geographic names and geographic subdivisions.*

Below is an extract from a LC subject heading and some of its subdivisions. Note the subject headings and geographical subdivisions generated.

**Architecture, Domestic** *(May Subd Geog)*

    UF   Domestic architecture

    BT   Architecture

    NT   A-frame houses

          Courtyard houses

            and so on . . .

  —**African influences**

  —**Conservation and restoration** *(May Subd Geog)*

  —**Mission style**

  —**Shingle style** *(May Subd Geog)*

**Subject headings generated, using 'Fiji' as a geographic subdivision:**

Architecture, Domestic

Architecture, Domestic—Fiji

Architecture, Domestic—African influences

Architecture, Domestic—Fiji—African influences

Architecture, Domestic—Conservation and restoration

Architecture, Domestic—Conservation and restoration—Fiji

Architecture, Domestic—Mission style

Architecture, Domestic—Fiji—Mission style

Architecture, Domestic—Shingle style

Architecture, Domestic—Shingle style—Fiji

 **EXERCISE 7.2**

*Write out all possible subdivisions of the LCSH entry given below, using **China** as a geographic subdivision. For example, 'Banks and banking—China'*

**Banks and banking** *(May Subd Geog)*

. . .

—**Automation**

——**Equipment and supplies**

—**Data processing**

——**Contracting out** *(May Subd Geog)*

. . .

—**Government ownership** *(May Subd Geog)*

——**Law and legislation** *(May Subd Geog)*

## Multiple Subdivisions (H 1090)

A multiple subdivision is a subdivision in LCSH that is used to suggest the creation of similar subdivisions under the heading. It is indicated by terms in square brackets generally followed by the word 'etc.' A multiple subdivision under a heading means any similar type of term to those in the square brackets can be used. Note, however, that the syntax must be the same.

 For the following heading with multiple subdivisions:
**World War, 1939-1945—Personal narratives, American, [French, German, etc.]**

Possible headings are
**World War, 1939-1945—Personal narratives, American**
**World War, 1939-1945—Personal narratives, Australian**
**World War, 1939-1945—Personal narratives, Dutch**
**World War, 1939-1945—Personal narratives, French**
**World War, 1939-1945—Personal narratives, German**   and so on,
*but not*
**World War, 1939-1945—Personal narratives, United States**
**World War, 1939-1945—Personal narratives, Australia**   etc

The functional equivalent of a multiple subdivision may be given as a scope note.

 For example,
**Solar eclipses**
Subdivided by date, e.g., Solar eclipses—1854

 **EXERCISE 7.3**
*Using LCSH, provide a subject heading for each of the following:*

| Topic | Subject heading |
|---|---|
| 1. Religious aspects of animal experiments from the Islamic viewpoint | _____ |
| 2. Subject headings for astronomy | _____ |
| 3. Christian beliefs about salt | _____ |
| 4. German words and phrases in the English Language | _____ |
| 5. Jewish aspects of codependency | _____ |

# CHAPTER EIGHT
# Free Floating Subdivisions and Pattern Headings

### Free-Floating Subdivisions (H1095)

The term 'free-floating subdivision' refers to form or topical subdivisions that could apply to many subject headings. In the interest of saving space, they are not listed under every heading for which they might be appropriate; instead lists are provided in the *Subject headings manual* and in the pdf file *LCSH free-floating subdivisions* http://www.loc.gov/aba/publications/FreeLCSH/SUBDIVISIONS.pdf. The cataloger may assign these subdivisions as required to various subject headings, without specific instructions from within LCSH.

 For example, for a resource concerning statistics on butterfly farming:

- *Butterfly farming* is a valid LCSH topical heading, but there is no subdivision for 'statistics' under that heading in LCSH
- nor is there a subdivision for 'butterfly farming' under the main heading *Statistics*
- however, the list of free-floating subdivisions indicates that —**Statistics** can be used with topical headings
- therefore, it is correct to assign the heading **Butterfly farming—Statistics.**

### Points to Note about Free-Floating Subdivisions

- They may not appear separately in the printed or online version.
- They must be used in accordance with the guidelines in the *Subject headings manual*.
- Not every free-floating subdivision may be used against every heading.
- Sometimes they are simply instructions under the subject heading they represent,

    for example,
    A monthly dental magazine is about dentistry, so the main topic is **Dentistry**. The item is also a periodical, and we want to incorporate this into our heading.

    The LCSH heading **Periodicals** provides the instruction:
    >      SA      *subdivision* Periodicals *under specific subjects, e.g.*
    >               Engineering—Periodicals;
    >               United States—History—Periodicals.

    So we can assign the subject heading:
    >               **Dentistry—Periodicals**.

    Note that —**Periodicals** is a free-floating subdivision.

## SEE ALSO and USE Statements for Free Floating Subdivisions

### *See also* (SA) references

*See also* references offer an alternative form of heading. Although the terminology seems to indicate that one can choose to use this alternative or not, this is not the case. *See also* statements give instructions on alternatives that **must** be used, provided all the conditions specified in the statement are met.

A *see also* statement often provides the authority to use a heading as a free floating subdivision. It defines the types of heading where the subdivision may be used.

 For example, I have an item about the migration of Maa people.

- LCSH contains a heading *Maa (Vietnamese people)* but no subdivision for 'migration'
- I look up *Migration* and find the heading *Migrations of nations* but no tie to the Maa
- however, under *Migrations of nations* is a SA reference which says '**SA** *subdivision* Migrations *under ethnic groups'*
- this provides the permission to use **—Migrations** under any heading which is an ethnic group of people
- therefore, I can assign the heading **Maa (Vietnamese people)—Migrations.**

### USE statements

If a particular subdivision cannot be used as a heading, sometimes a **USE** statement will provide permission to use the non-allowed heading as a free floating subdivision.

 For example, I have an item about animal housing in hot weather.

- *Animal housing* is a valid LCSH heading but provides no subdivision for 'hot weather'
- *Hot weather conditions* says "**USE** *subdivision* Hot weather conditions *under topical headings*
- Therefore, I can assign the heading **Animal housing—Hot weather conditions.**

Before using a free-floating subdivision, always check LCSH to ensure the heading you plan to use does not include a subdivision that covers the same concept using a different term. In such cases, always use the subdivisions provided under a heading in preference to free-floating subdivisions.

 *Only use a subdivision from the free-floating subdivision lists if no appropriate subdivision is available under the LCSH heading you wish to use.*

A complete list of free-floating subdivisions is found in section H1095 in the *Subject headings manual*. Free-floating subdivisions can be topical, form or chronological; and some can be subdivided geographically. Information about these aspects, as well as scope notes and cross-references for each entry, are included in the *Subject headings manual* list. The list, without scope notes or instructions, has been reproduced at the back of this book.

**EXERCISE 8.1**

*Are the following subject headings and subdivisions correctly established?  If not, why not?*

| Headings | Correct/ Incorrect | Reason and correct form (if incorrect) |
|---|---|---|
| 1.  Dentistry—Law and legislation | | |
| 2.  Buildings—Maintenance | | |
| 3.  Buildings—Maintenance and repair | | |
| 4.  Books —Reviews—Periodicals | | |
| 5.  Dentistry—Book reviews | | |
| 6.  Real property—Finance, personal | | |
| 7.  Chicago (Ill.)—Appropriations and expenditure | | |
| 8.  Chamber music—Early works to 1800—England | | |
| 9.  Paper industry—History | | |
| 10.   Parachutes—Testing— Equipment—Certification— United States | | |

## EXERCISE 8.2

*Using LCSH, allocate suitable subject headings to the following. Include one or more subdivisions to make your heading more specific.*

| Topic | Subject heading |
|---|---|
| 1. Bibliography on plant migration | |
| 2. Colonisation of Zimbabwe | |
| 3. Pensions of bus drivers in Mexico | |
| 4. History of the laws regulating collection agencies in New Zealand | |
| 5. Satirical cartoons of nurses | |
| 6. Laboratories for sensory evaluation in Geneva | |
| 7. Diagnosis of mouth cancer in Glasgow | |
| 8. Testing of instruments used in nuclear power plants in Tokyo | |
| 9. Deterioration of murals in Venice | |
| 10. Chinese coiffures in the 18th century | |

## Pattern Headings

### Introduction

There are some topical or form subdivisions that would be useful for a particular category of subject headings, but cannot be assigned across the entire LCSH scheme. For example, all the activities associated with crops—seeds, sowing, fertilization, weeding, harvesting, eating, etc.—are useful subdivisions under any type of crop, but they would not be useful subdivisions under types of motor vehicles!

To avoid repeating these subdivisions under all possible subject headings in their category, only one (or sometimes a few) headings from the category are chosen, and all the possible subdivisions for that category are listed under those representative headings in LCSH. These headings form *patterns* for other headings in their category. In this way they are a form of free-floating subdivision.

The *Subject headings manual* lists the free-floating subdivisions controlled by pattern headings (H 1146-H 1200). H1146 gives an overview of all the categories and their pattern headings; the sections following (H 1147-H 1200) list each category in turn, with subdivisons that can be used with that category.

Pattern subdivisions are incorporated into the general list of free-floating subdivisions in the online version of LCSH, and many are also in the pdf lists of free-floating subdivisions. However, on some occasions when the pattern is confined to a particular usage they may not be in these more general lists. It may be necessary to consult H 1095, H 1100, the list of free-floating subdivisions used under classes of persons and H 1105, the list of free-floating sub-divisions used under corporate bodies, in addition to a specific pattern heading list when constructing subject headings with free-floating subdivisions.

Pattern headings have not been designated for all possible categories in the world of knowledge. Not all headings in the LCSH system are covered by pattern headings. Therefore, it is important to understand what pattern headings are, and how they work, to ensure the most appropriate heading is assigned.

## Using Pattern Headings

### General rule

Use any subdivision that is established under a pattern heading as a free-floating subdivision with any other heading belonging to its category, as long as it is appropriate and no conflicting heading is established in the subject authority file.

### Procedure

1. Find the correct form of the main heading.
2. Check LCSH under the subject heading for the desired subdivision. If found, stop here.
3. If not found, check the list of free-floating subdivisions, or check for a free-floater as a heading.

4. If a useful subdivision is still not found, check the list of Pattern Headings to find an appropriate category. Do not use a heading at the broader 'category' level (representing a class of items); find the actual subject heading/s used for that category.

5. Note: If two or more pattern headings are designated to represent a category, a subdivision established under any of these headings may be used as free-floating for a heading in that category if it is appropriate.

6. Once the correct pattern heading is located, use any of the subdivisions as required.

 For example,

| | |
|---|---|
| *Title* | Drought resistance of rice in Thailand |

*Procedure*

1. Main heading is **Rice,** but no appropriate subdivision is found.
2. No free-floating subdivision is suitable.
3. Look for the Pattern Heading category. 'Rice' belongs to the category 'Plants and crops'. The pattern heading for this category is **Corn**.
4. Go to **Corn** in LCSH and look for a suitable subdivision. Note: all instructions that apply to this heading (e.g., *May Subd Geog)* also apply to the heading you have selected.
5. Choose the subdivision 'drought tolerance'.

*Subject heading* **Rice—Drought tolerance—Thailand**

## Subdivisions Controlled by Pattern Headings (H 1146)

These charts show the pattern headings established to date, as listed in H 1146 of the *Subject headings manual*. They are arranged first by major discipline ('Subject Field'), then by category and heading. The final column indicates the section of the *Subject headings manual* that lists all the subdivisions for that category.

| Subject Field | Category | Pattern Heading(s) | |
|---|---|---|---|
| **THE ARTS** | Art | Art, Italian<br>Art, Chinese<br>Art, Japanese<br>Art, Korean | H 1148 |
| | Groups of literary authors *(including authors, poets, dramatists, etc.)* | Authors, English | H 1155.2 |
| | Literary works entered under author | Shakespeare, William, 1564-1616. Hamlet | H 1155.6 |
| | Literary works entered under title | Beowulf | H 1155.8 |
| | Languages and groups of languages | English language<br>French language<br>Romance languages | H 1154 |
| | Literatures *(including individual genres)* | English literature | H 1156 |
| | Music compositions | Operas | H 1160 |
| | Musical instruments | Piano<br>Clarinet<br>Violin | H 1161 |

| Subject Field | Category | Pattern Heading(s) | |
|---|---|---|---|
| **HISTORY AND GEOGRAPHY** | Colonies of individual countries | Great Britain-Colonies | H 1149.5 |
| | Legislative bodies *(including individual chambers)* | United States. Congress | H 1155 |
| | Military services *(including armies, navies, marines, etc.)* | United States-Armed Forces<br>United States. Air Force<br>United States. Army<br>United States. Marine Corps<br>United States. Navy | H 1159 |
| | Wars | World War, 1939-1945<br>United States-History-Civil War, 1861-1865 | H 1200 |

| Subject Field | Category | Pattern Heading(s) | |
|---|---|---|---|
| **RELIGION** | Religious and monastic orders | Jesuits | H 1186 |
| | Religions | Buddhism | H 1185 |
| | Christian denominations | Catholic Church | II 1187 |
| | Sacred works *(including parts)* | Bible | H 1188 |

| Subject Field | Category | Pattern Heading(s) | |
|---|---|---|---|
| **SCIENCE AND TECHNOLOGY** | Land vehicles | Automobiles | H 1195 |
| | Materials | Concrete | H 1158 |
| | | Metals | |
| | Chemicals | Copper | H 1149 |
| | | Insulin | |
| | Organs and regions of the body | Heart | H 1164 |
| | | Foot | |
| | Diseases | Cancer | H 1150 |
| | | Tuberculosis | |
| | Plants and crops | Corn | H 1180 |
| | Animals | Fishes | H 1147 |
| | | Cattle | |

| Subject Field | Category | Pattern Heading(s) | |
|---|---|---|---|
| **SOCIAL SCIENCES** | Industries | Construction industry | H 1153 |
| | | Retail trade | |
| | Types of educational institutions | Universities and colleges | H 1151.5 |
| | Individual educational institutions | Harvard University | H 1151 |
| | Legal topics | Labor laws and legislation | H 1154.5 |

**EXERCISE 8.3**

*Using LCSH, find appropriate subject headings for the following. Record the pattern heading used.*

| Topic | Pattern heading | Heading |
|---|---|---|
| 1. The lifecycle of the chipmunk | | |
| 2. Vaccinating cats | | |
| 3. Ellipsis in Albanian | | |
| 4. The psychotropic effects of iodine | | |
| 5. Economic conditions of Dutch colonies in Asia | | |
| 6. Breeding lions | | |
| 7. Origins of Zen Buddhism in Japan | | |
| 8. Anti-lock brake systems for dune buggies | | |
| 9. How drugs affect the brain | | |
| 10. Regional variations in the macadamia nut industry (hint: this is an industry) | | |
| 11. Production standards of films adapted from Arabic children's stories | | |
| 12. Research on methods of painting of plastics | | |
| 13. How French has had an impact on English | | |
| 14. Genetic engineering of sheep in New Zealand | | |
| 15. How to fix vapour lock problems in buses | | |

### EXERCISE 8.4

*Are the following subject headings correct? If not, indicate a possible correct heading.*

| Topic | Subject heading |
|---|---|
| 1. Liver—Size | _____ |
| 2. Canada. Parliament—Duties of members | _____ |
| 3. Spring wheat—Diseases and pests—Italy — Biological control | _____ |
| 4. Chinese-French War, 1884-1885—Battles | _____ |
| 5. Guitar—Strings—Materials | _____ |
| 6. Dogs—Embryos—Canada—Transplantation | _____ |
| 7. Llamas—Peru—Handling | _____ |
| 8. Toes, Dislocation of | _____ |
| 9. Ranunculus—Time of flowering | _____ |
| 10. Canola—Disease and pest resistance—Genetic aspects | _____ |

# CHAPTER NINE
## Geographic Names and Subdivisions

Place names (jurisdictional and non-jurisdictional), including geographic features, areas and regions, city sections, early cities, empires, kingdoms, etc. may all be used as name headings in LCSH.

## Geographic Names

Geographic names are used in subject cataloging as:
- Headings, e.g., **Scotland—Description and travel**
- Subdivisions, e.g., **Corn—New South Wales**
- Qualifiers, e.g., **Corinthian Hall (Kansas City, Mo.)**
- Part of an adjectival or inverted heading, e.g., **French drama; Dramatists, French**

Geographic names generally fall into two categories:
- Names for political jurisdictions (using the name of the geographic area to represent the name of the government). In this category are included names of countries, provinces, states, cities and towns.

   For example,
  > **South Dakota**
  > **Canada**
  > **Victoria**

- Names for areas that are not covered by a political jurisdiction. In this category are included names of natural geographic features and built structures.

   For example,
  > **Australia, Southeastern**
  > **Great Barrier Reef (Qld.)**
  > **Mississippi River**
  > **Golden Gate Bridge (San Francisco, Calif.)**

## Jurisdictional Name Headings
### General rules
- Use only the latest name of a jurisdiction as long as the territorial identity remains essentially unchanged. For example, although both Ceylon and Sri Lanka are valid name headings, only Sri Lanka is used in subject cataloging (*Subject headings manual*, H 708).
- For situations where jurisdictions have merged or split, various headings may be appropriate depending on the area and time period discussed. In general, assign subject headings that correspond to the physical extent of the area being discussed.
- If additions are required to place names, use parentheses.

- Add a word or phrase commonly used to distinguish between identical place names.
    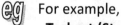 For example,
    **Tarbert (Strathclyde, Scotland)**
    **Tarbert (Western Isles, Scotland)**

- Give the name of an appropriate smaller place before the name of the specified larger place if necessary to identify the place (as in the case of a community within a city).
     For example,
    **Hyde Park (Chicago, Ill.)**
    **Chelsea (London, England)**

- If the first part of a place name is a term indicating a type of jurisdiction, and the place is commonly listed under another element of its name in lists published in the language of the country in which it is located, omit the term indicating the type of jurisdiction.
     For example,
    **Kerry (Ireland)**
    *not*
    **County Kerry (Ireland)**

- In all other cases, include the jurisdictional term.
     For example,
    **Colonia Condesa (Mexico City, Mexico)**

## Non-Jurisdictional Name Headings
A range of named entities can be established as headings. These include:
    Ancient cities
    Archaeological sites, historic sites, etc.
    Areas and regions (when not free-floating)
    Boundary lines
    Bridges
    Canals
    City sections
    Dams
    Farms, ranches, gardens
    Forests, grasslands, etc.
    Geologic basins, geologic formations, etc.
    Mines
    Parks, reserves, refuges, recreation areas, etc.
    Reservoirs
    Roads, streets, trails
    Tunnels

and geographic features including

| | | |
|---|---|---|
| basins | gorges | plateaus |
| bays | gulfs | rivers |
| canyons | lagoons | seas |
| capes | lakes | sounds |
| caves | moors | steppes |
| creeks | mountains | straits |
| deserts | ocean currents | tonal islands |
| falls | peninsulas | |
| fjords | plains | |

Instructions regarding geographic name headings are given in various sections of the *Subject headings manual* between H 690 and H 1055. For non-jurisdictional headings in particular, H069 discusses how to formulate headings for named non-jurisdictional features, H 760 deals with geographic regions, H 800 and 807 discuss rivers, valleys, watershed and islands, and H 405 lists which geographic features are given MARC 11x tags (as names) and which have MARC 15x tags (as subjects).

## Geographic Headings That Are Qualified (H 810)

Geographic qualifiers are additions to a place name, enclosed in parentheses, indicating the broader jurisdiction in which the place is located. Most places used as subject headings are qualified (rare exceptions being geographic features that span a number of jurisdictions, e.g., river systems).

Always qualify by the name of the jurisdiction (i.e, the country name) **except for the following countries**:

| | |
|---|---|
| Australia | use names of states |
| Canada | use names of provinces |
| Great Britain | use names of constituent countries |
| Malaysia | use names of states ** |
| United States | use names of states |

For a full list of the political divisions for these exceptions, and the forms to be used as qualifiers (i.e., abbreviations and spellings), see the *Subject headings manual* H 810.

** Malaysia is only qualified using the names of states at the 'Main Heading' level; e.g., **Kuching (Sarawak, Malaysia)—History**. When using Malaysia's constituent states as subdivisions (see the next section of this chapter for details of geographic subdivisions), one reverts to the 'normal' format for geographic subdivisions, e.g., *<topic>—Malaysia—Kuching*. For discussion of the use of geographic areas as direct and indirect subdivisions, and the exceptions to these rules, see the *Subject Headings Manual* section H 830.

### EXERCISE 9.1

*Using LCSH, establish the correct headings for the following geographic features.*

| Topic | Subject heading |
|---|---|
| 1.  Kythnos Island | |
| 2.  Isle Royale National Park | |
| 3.  Royal National Park (near Sydney, New South Wales, Australia) | |
| 4.  Central Park (in New York) | |
| 5.  Statue of Liberty | |
| 6.  Grand Canyon | |
| 7.  Tower Hamlets Cemetery (London) | |
| 8.  Merri River | |
| 9.  London River (in France) | |
| 10.  Amazon River | |
| 11.  Death Valley | |
| 12.  St. Patrick's Street (Ireland) | |
| 13.  17th Street in Washington | |
| 14.  Highway 40 (United States) | |
| 15.  Hilo Bay | |
| 16.  Pearl Bridge (in Japan) | |
| 17.  Ayers Rock National Park | |
| 18.  Mount Whitney in California | |
| 19.  The Vatican | |
| 20.  Wailing Wall (in Jerusalem) | |
| 21.  Hyde Park in Sydney, Australia | |

## Geographic Subdivisions

Place names may also be used as *subdivisions* in LCSH. There are two forms of geographic subdivision—direct and indirect—so-called because of where the largest geographic entity is placed within the subdivision.

## Direct Geographic Subdivisions

### General rule

If a geographic subdivision is at the country level or above, the name of the place *directly* follows the main heading or subdivision at the instruction *(May Subd Geog)*

 For example,

**Futurism (Art)—France**

**Health occupations students—Mexico**

**Geology—Antarctica.**

In addition, first order political divisions in these areas also follow the topical element directly:

| | |
|---|---|
| Canada | provinces |
| United States | states |
| Great Britain | constituent countries (i.e., England, Wales, Scotland, Northern Ireland) |
| Australia | states and territories *(note: this is a local exception to LCSH rules. It is an option for Australian libraries, only used in Australian cataloging)* |

 For example,

**Health occupations students—British Columbia**

**Railroads—Scotland**

**Geology—New South Wales** *(for Australian cataloging)*

## Indirect Geographic Subdivisions

### General rule

In many cases, the name of a larger geographic entity is placed before the name of a more specific locality. This is described as assigning the place name *indirectly*.

 *Places below national level are normally assigned indirectly.*

Generally, the name of the country is interposed between the topic and the subordinate political or geographic division.

 For example,

**Labor supply—France—Paris**

*instead of*

Labor supply—Paris

**Litter (Trash)—Italy—Venice**
> *instead of*
Litter (Trash)—Venice

**Narcotic clinics—Thailand—Bangkok**
> *instead of*
Narcotic clinics—Bangkok

*And for libraries outside Australia:*
> **Geology—Australia—New South Wales**
>> *instead of*
> Geology—New South Wales

## Exception

For places in Canada, the United States, Great Britain and Australia*, interpose the name of the first-order political division (rather than the name of the country) between the topic and the subordinate political or geographic division.

    For example,
**Labor supply—California—Los Angeles**
> *not*
Labor supply—United States—Los Angeles

**Narcotic clinics—Scotland—Glasgow**
> *not*
Narcotic clinics—Great Britain—Glasgow

*In Australia:*
**Litter (Trash)—New South Wales—Sydney**
*In other parts of the world:*
**Litter (Trash)—Australia—Sydney (N.S.W.)**

*\* The use of Australia as an exception to the general rule is used by the National Library of Australia and libraries that contribute to the Australian national network, Libraries Australia.*

    To summarise:

Put the geographic name directly after the main heading if it is:
- a country name
- larger than a country e.g., Europe, Middle East
- in more than one country e.g., a mountain range, large body of water, region
- one of the Canadian provinces
- one of the USA states

- one of the four countries of Britain – England, Wales, Scotland, Northern Ireland
- one of the Australian states *(only if cataloging in Australia)*

**Examples**

        &lt;topic&gt;—China

        &lt;topic&gt;—England

        &lt;topic&gt;—British Columbia

        &lt;topic&gt;—Utah

        &lt;topic&gt;—Queensland *(if cataloging in Australia)*

**but not**

        &lt;topic&gt;—Bavaria (a German State)

        &lt;topic&gt;—London

        &lt;topic&gt;—Ural Mountains

All smaller places have the country inserted between the topic and the place name:

        &lt;topic&gt;—Italy—Rome

        &lt;topic&gt;—France—Paris

        &lt;topic&gt;—Turkey—Taurus Mountains

*Except* for places wholly within:

- Canadian provinces
- USA states
- The four countries of Great Britain: England, Wales, Scotland, Northern Ireland
- Australian states *(only if cataloging in Australia)*

For these exceptions, insert the province, state or constituent country between the topic and the place name, for example:

        &lt;topic&gt;—California—Los Angeles

        &lt;topic&gt;—England—London

        &lt;topic&gt;—Queensland—Brisbane *(if cataloging in Australia)*

 ***The first geographical subdivision should be a country or one of the exceptions. The second geographical subdivision should not be smaller than a city.***

## Position of Geographic Subdivisions

We mentioned in Chapter 7 that the geographic subdivision follows the last element that can be divided by place (that is, which contains the designation *(May Subd Geog)*).

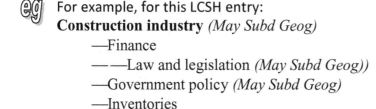

For example, for this LCSH entry:

**Construction industry** *(May Subd Geog)*

        —Finance

        — —Law and legislation *(May Subd Geog))*

        —Government policy *(May Subd Geog)*

        —Inventories

the heading for a work on law and legislation in the construction industry in Indonesia is
**Construction industry—Finance—Law and legislation—Indonesia**

while the heading for a work on inventories in the construction industry in Indonesia is
**Construction industry—Indonesia—Inventories.**

 **EXERCISE 9.2**

*Using LCSH, allocate suitable subject headings to the following. Include one or more subdivisions to make your heading more specific.*

| Topic | Subject heading |
|---|---|
| 1.  Diseases of the eyelids in China | |
| 2.  Diseases of the limbs in Africa | |
| 3.  Taxation of show business personalities in Venezuela | |
| 4.  The labelling of bread in Montréal | |
| 5.  The legislation on bread labelling in Nova Scotia | |
| 6.  Abnormalities of cattle in Argentina | |
| 7.  Collective agreements in the airlines in Belgium | |
| 8.  Job stress in health professionals in Singapore | |
| 9.  A report on kumara plant pests in Bali (a province of Indonesia) | |
| 10. Historical monuments in Ballarat, Victoria | |

## Treatment of Cities

LCSH uses two forms of headings for names of cities, depending on whether the city is used as a main heading or as a subdivision.

**When cities are main headings:**

- Use the format **<city> (<country>)** e.g., Rome (Italy)
- For the 'exception' countries (USA, Canada, Great Britain, Malaysia, Australia) use the format **<city> (<state or province>)** e.g., Los Angeles (Calif.); London (England); *or if cataloging in Australia,* Sydney (N.S.W.)

Use this format if the work is about the city in general, or the city with some topical or chronological subdivisions, e.g.,

| | |
|---|---|
| Paris (France) | Paris (France)—Race relations |
| Vancouver (B.C.) | Vancouver (B.C.)—Social life and customs |

**When cities are subdivisions of topical main headings:**

- Use the format **<topic>—<country>—<city>** e.g., Birds—Italy—Rome
- For the 'exception' countries (USA, Canada, Great Britain, Australia) use the format **<topic>—<state or province>—<city>** e.g., Birds—Glasgow—Scotland

Note that when you use state or province jurisdictions as part of a subdivision, you don't use abbreviations. Instead, spell out the full name of the state, province or constituent country.

> Birds—California—Los Angeles
> Police—England—Liverpool
> Education—British Columbia—Vancouver

Use this chart to remember the different ways LCSH treats cities.

| LCSH Treatment of Cities | | |
|---|---|---|
| | **As a Main Heading** | **As a Subdivision** |
| **For most of the World** | *City (Country)*<br>e.g., Paris (France) | *Topic—Country—City*<br>e.g., Birds—France—Paris |
| **For USA, Canada, Great Britain, Malaysia** (for main headings only), **Australia** (in Australia only) | *City (State)*<br>*or*<br>*City (Province, etc)*<br>e.g., Chicago (Ill.)<br>London (England)<br>Ipoh (Perak, Malaysia)<br>Melbourne (Vic.) | *Topic—State—City*<br>*or*<br>*Topic—Province, etc—City*<br>e.g., Birds—Illinois—Chicago<br>Birds—England—London<br>Birds—Victoria—Melbourne |

**EXERCISE 9.3**

*The following are valid LCSH subject headings, but the format for the city name is incorrect. Use the correct format in each heading.*

| Incorrect | Correct |
|---|---|
| 1. Artists—Beijing | |
| 2. Phoenix—Telephone directories | |
| 3. Museums—Phoenix | |
| 4. Peonies—Tokyo | |
| 5. Hanoi—Aerial views | |
| 6. Soccer—Hanoi | |
| 7. Cairo—Economic conditions | |
| 8. Berlin—Statistics | |
| 9. Flea markets—Mexico City—Directories | |
| 10. Surfing—Sydney | |
| 11. Cheese—Copenhagen | |
| 12. Toronto—Maps | |
| 13. Restaurants—Toronto—Guidebooks | |
| 14. Bedding—Suva | |
| 15. Tombs—Decoration—New Delhi | |

**EXERCISE 9.4**

*Using LCSH, provide subject headings for the following topics, including geographic subdivisions.*

| Topic | Subject heading |
|---|---|
| 1. American libraries | _____ |
| 2. Hospitals in Albuquerque, New Mexico, USA | _____ |
| 3. A field guide to birds around Billings in Montana, USA | _____ |
| 4. Laws regulating online gambling in the Eastern Mediterranean | _____ |
| 5.   A report on the police in Utah, USA | _____ |
| 6. Body surfing on the Gold Coast of Queensland (in Australia) | _____ |
| 7. Black colleges in the United States | _____ |
| 8. Australian badgers (Vombatidae) of the south-eastern region of Australia | _____ |
| 9. Art colonies in Banff, Canada | _____ |
| 10. Art colonies in Kuala Lumpor, Malaysia | _____ |
| 11. Traditional Spanish folk beliefs | _____ |
| 12. Painters from Rocksprings, Wyoming, USA | _____ |
| 13. Research into the climate of Darwin, NT (in Australia) | _____ |
| 14. Bridges in Rome (in Italy) | _____ |
| 15. Walking in Cardiff (in Britain) | _____ |

# CHAPTER TEN
# Names

## Names as Subject Headings
The following types of names can be used as subject headings:

- **personal names**, including names of groups of legendary, mythological and fictitious characters, gods etc.
- **family names**, including dynasties and royal houses
- **place names** (jurisdictional and non-jurisdictional), including geographic features areas and regions, city sections, early cities, empires, kingdoms, etc.
- **names of corporate bodies**
- **names of art works**
- **names of chemicals, drugs and minerals**
- **biological names**
- other names, e.g., languages (including computer languages), ethnic groups, roads, structures, buildings, railroads, projects, movements, events, trade names, games.

This table illustrates the range of names found in LCSH:

| Category | Example of Heading |
|---|---|
| PEOPLE | |
| individuals | García Márquez, Gabriel, 1927-2014 |
| families, dynasties | Luce family |
| cartoon & fictitious characters, legends, imaginary people | Felix the Cat (Fictitious character) |
| PLACES | |
| jurisdictional (follows government borders) | New Zealand |
| non-jurisdictional | Great Bear Lake (N.W.T.) |
| CORPORATE BODIES | Societas Europeas |
| ART WORKS | Blue Poles |
| CHEMICALS, DRUGS , MINERALS | Oxygen, Penicillin, Gold |
| BIOLOGICAL NAMES | Cephalopoda, Leucanthemum vulgare |
| LANGUAGES | German language, PASCAL |

| ROADS, BUILDINGS, ETC | King's Highway (Jordan) |
|---|---|
| EVENTS | Holi (Hindu festival) |
| MOVEMENTS | Anti-slavery League |
| GAMES | Monopoly (Game) |

## Finding Name Headings

Not all name headings are in LCSH. Personal names, names of corporate bodies, jurisdictional names, and uniform titles are only included in the subject headings list if they require special treatment or if they have unique subdivisions attached.

In all other cases, names consisting of proper nouns are recorded in name authority files. The *Subject headings manual* section H 405 provides guidance on what sorts of names will be found in LCSH and the LC Subject Authorities, and what will be in Library of Congress Name Authorities.

To find name headings, search the following (in this order)
- LCSH, to see if the name has been included
- Your library's own authority file, in case you have used the heading before
- A large well-respected authority file, either international (*LC Name Authorities, WorldCat Authorities,* or *VIAF—Virtual International Authority File*), national (*Libraries Australia Authorities*), or belonging to a regional network.

If a named entity is the topic of a resource, it should be used as a subject heading even if the name is not listed in LCSH. In such cases, try to use the form of name established in an existing authority file. As a final resort, set up a new name authority using the cataloging guidelines in *Resource Description and Access* (RDA) or the older *Anglo-American Cataloguing Rules* (AACR2).

## Qualified Names

Names, like any LCSH heading, may be simple or inverted. For many names it will be necessary to differentiate between persons or items bearing the same name, or where the meaning of the name is not obvious. In these cases, the names are qualified by an explanatory term.

Names may be qualified:
- By category
    - P-40 (Fighter planes)
    - DDT (Insecticide)
    - Queen (Chess)

- By place
    Hyde Park (London, England)
    Hyde Park (Chicago, Ill.)
    Andasolos Cave (Mexico)
- By date or other personal characteristic
    - Lincoln, Abraham, 1809-1865
- Or by a combination of terms (with geographic qualifiers last)
    Questacon (Building, Canberra, A.C.T.)

## Assigning Name Headings

 **Tip 1.** *Always use authority files.*
If you do not find the name as a subject in LCSH, check a name authority file.

 **Tip 2.** *Names may only be divided by subdivisions which are:*
- in LCSH, if the name is given as a main heading
- free-floating subdivisions, whether the name is listed in LCSH or not
- pattern headings, whether the name is listed in LCSH or not.

 **Tip 3.** *If a subject heading is the same as a descriptive heading, use both.*
Refer to LCSH's guideline on *'Assigning a subject heading if it is the same as another access point'* (H 180) in Chapter 5 of this book.

## Personal Names—Biography  (H 1330)

Biography refers to the genre of works consisting of the life histories of individuals, whether written by the individual themselves or by others.
- *Individual biography* refers to a work about the life of one individual.
- *Collective biography* refers to a work about the lives of two or more persons.
- A *complete biography* is a work about the life span of one person.
- A *partial biography* gives only some details about a person's life.
- An *autobiography* is written by the individuals themselves.

Do not consider a work a biography simply because it provides a short summary or chronology of someone's life. In order to be considered a biography, a work should present personal details of the biographee in at least 50% of the available space. Personal details of birth, education, marriage, personal habits and experiences, death and so on should be synthesized and presented as a whole.

The biography or autobiography of a person requires the use of a personal name subject heading. However, LCSH does this by using two separate headings: a separate heading for the name of the person, and an additional heading or headings for the class of person, with the subdivision '—Biography'.

**General rules**

- Assign to any biographical work, whether individual or collective, a combination of the following types of headings :
  - *<Name or names of persons discussed>*
  - *<Class of persons to which the persons discussed belong>—Biography*, or *<Class of person>—<Place>—Biography*
  - additional headings for organization, ethnic group, place, event, gender
  - additional specific topics, as appropriate.
- Use the subdivision **—Biography** to designate individual and collective biography, autobiography, personal reminiscences and personal narratives.
- Do not subdivide the name heading for a person by the subdivision **—Biography**. Simply use the correct form of the personal name as a separate subject heading.
- Assign name headings (usually only 3-4) for persons discussed. If a collective biography discusses more than 3-4 persons, do not allocate individual name subject headings. (see additional notes on collective biographies in the section below)
- Use the personal name for a head of state or other official, not the 'corporate head of state' heading.
- Use subdivisions from the free-floating subdivisions or pattern headings lists. Any appropriate free-floating subdivision under names of persons (H 1110) may be applied.
  - For subdivisions of literary works entered under author, use the pattern heading: *Shakespeare, William, 1564-1616. Hamlet.*
  - For subdivisions of literary works entered under title, use the pattern heading: *Beowolf*
- Assign headings for the subject area or activity that the person is associated with: *<Class of person> — <Place> —Biography*

   For example,
  **Plumbers—Maryland—Biography**
- If a person belongs to several classes of persons (for example, a sportsman turned company director who later became a politician), use multiple *'<class of person>—Biography'* headings, one for each class.
- Allocate additional headings where possible to bring out any of the following subject aspects:
  organization
  ethnic group
  place
  event
  gender

For example, for a resource on the life of Cathy Freeman, an Aboriginal Australian runner who won a gold medal at the Sydney Olympic Games in 2000:

1. Begin by establishing her name in a name authority file: **Freeman, Cathy, 1973—**
2. Indicate her main class of person, and place of activity: **Athletes—Australia—Biography**
3. Add an additional heading for ethnic group, since her aboriginality was a significant aspect of the resource's coverage: **Aboriginal Australians—Biography**
4. Add headings for named events that were significant, again using an established heading from a name authority file: **Olympic Games (27th : 2000 : Sydney, N.S.W)**
5. Add additional significant topics as appropriate: **Athletics—Australia**

The subject headings assigned to this resource would be:
> **Freeman, Cathy, 1973—**
> **Athletes—Australia—Biography**
> **Aboriginal Australians—Biography**
> **Olympic Games (27th : 2000 : Sydney, N.S.W.)**
> **Athletics—Australia**

**Partial biography**

Partial biographies are works that deal with individuals but are less than 50% biographical. Examples of this type of work are critical works about individual artists, literary authors, philosophers, theologians, etc. which focus on their work more than their life, as well as works about the life and times of individual statesmen or rulers in which there is more about the history of the time than the life of the ruler.

If the work treats the life of an individual as one aspect of a fuller treatment, look for personal biographical details of approximately 20%, even if the complete life history is not included. If a personal biography of 20% is not present, still include the name of the person but do not allocate biographical headings.

 For example,

| | |
|---|---|
| *Title* | The personal life of wartime generals |
| *Subject headings* | 1. Patton, George S. (George Smith), 1885-1945 |
| | 2. World War, 1939-1945 |
| | 3. Generals—United States |
| | 4. United States. Army |

**Collective biography**

A collective biography covers the lives of a number of people.
- For 2-4 people covered, assign name headings and *<Class of person>—Biography* headings for each person.
- For more than four persons covered in a collective biography, assign *<Class of person>—Biography* headings only.

- Use *Biography* as a main heading (not a subdivision) for a collective biography that is not about a particular type of person or topic, e.g., a general dictionary of biography or a list of biographies.
- Use *Biography-<Time period>* as a heading for a collective biography covering a specific time period, whether it is about types of persons or not.

  *eg*   For example, for a work titled *Famous people of the 19*[th] *century*, assign the heading:

    **Biography—19**[th] **Century**

  For a biographical dictionary of 20th century artists, assign the headings:

    **Artists—Biography—Dictionaries**
    **Biography—20**[th] **Century**

**EXERCISE 10.1**

*Using an authority file, provide a name subject heading for each of the following:*

| Topic | Subject heading |
|---|---|
| 1. Shakespeare | |
| 2. Antonia Byatt | |
| 3. T.S. Eliot | |
| 4. Joan of Arc | |
| 5. Queen Elizabeth II | |
| 6. The Tower of London | |
| 7. Empire State Building | |
| 8. Augustus Agar | |
| 9. The Tyree Family | |
| 10. Immanuel Kant | |

**EXERCISE 10.2**

*Using LCSH, provide appropriate subject headings including subdivisions for the following. You may need to check an authority file for the verified forms of names:*

| Topic | Subject heading |
|---|---|
| 1. Biography of Earl Warren, a governor of California | _____ |
| 2. Biography of American singer Tony Bennett | _____ |
| 3. A collective biography of the last 10 Prime Ministers of Canada and the events that took place during their tenure | _____ |
| 4. The history of the Pulitzer Prize | _____ |
| 5. The history of the Taylor family | _____ |
| 6. Biography of Lachlan Macquarie, a governor of New South Wales | _____ |
| 7. Biography of the Australian writer Patrick White | _____ |

# CHAPTER ELEVEN
## Subject Authority Files

### Introduction

**Authority control** is the maintenance of standard forms of headings in the catalog, so that library users can locate information using consistent subject, name and title headings. It also ensures that all future additions to the catalog use the same heading as an access point.

An **authority file** is the record of the correct form of names, series, subjects or uniform titles used in a catalog. It represents a record of decisions made by the cataloger in accordance with the library's policy. It records the standard form of a heading as prescribed by the current cataloging rules *Resource description and access* (RDA), and all references made to and from the headings.

One of the largest authority files is *Library of Congress authorities*, publicly available online at http://authorities.loc.gov. It includes subject, name, title and name/title authorities, each searched separately. While many countries use and contribute to these authority files, some augment the files with their own country-based headings. For example, *Canadian subject headings* (CHS) is an online subject authority file focusing on Canadian topics at http://www.bac-lac.gc.ca/eng/services/canadian-subject-headings/Pages/canadian-subject-headings.aspx. It is complemented by the name and title file *Canadiana authorities* https://www.collectionscanada.gc.ca/canadiana-authorities/index/index?lang=eng. *Libraries Australia authorities* is a subscription service available as part of the Libraries Australia network. Its subject authority file is based on LCSH, but includes additional Australian terms which have been approved by the National Library as '*Australian extensions to LCSH*' http://www.nla.gov.au/librariesaustralia/services/cataloguing/standards/lcsh-extension/.

The *Virtual international authority file* (VIAF) combines multiple authority files into a single service, hosted by OCLC and available online at http://viaf.org. It matches and links widely-used authority files from approximately 50 large or national libraries around the world. The VIAF is a developing project. At this stage, it covers name authorities (corporate, personal and geographic names), bibliographic titles, and Work and Expression authorities, but not subject authorities.

A **subject authority file** is a file of all the subject headings used in the catalog. It also contains references made to the headings. This controls the library's use of subject headings and ensures collocation of records that have the same access point.

An **authority record** is a separate record for each heading. It contains the correct form of the heading, references and notes relating to the reference source used to verify the name.

Two sorts of headings appear in a subject authority file:
- authorized headings or *preferred terms* that appear in the catalog only
- unauthorized headings or *non-preferred terms* with a USE reference to the preferred term.

Catalogers normally
1. check for headings used in their catalog
2. if the heading is not found, check an external authority file e.g., *LC authorities*
3. check the subject list (e.g., LCSH), and if not found construct the required heading
4. perform authority work to include the new heading and any references or links to other headings in the authority file.


## Creating Subject Authority Records

Many libraries do not create new subject headings or develop new subject authority records; they prefer to use existing LCSH headings and if available local country extensions to LCSH. However, it is useful for catalogers to understand what they see in an authority record, and know how to read and create one.

Like subject heading lists, authority records contain: headings; scope notes; broader, narrower and related terms; and non-preferred (Used For) terms. They can also contain information on sources used to determine the heading (the MARC21 Authority field 670, 'Source data found').

The following procedures for establishing a subject authority record take you through the range of references used in an online subject authority file, with the associated MARC coding. Authority records are created using a special MARC format, *MARC21 format for authority data*, which differs from the *MARC21 format for bibliographic data*. The MARC authority format is found at http://www.loc.gov/marc/authority/.

Bear in mind that you may not have to use all the references in the subject headings list. Libraries vary in the extent to which references are made, and the cataloger should always follow the library's cataloging policy.

**Procedures for creating a subject authority record**
The procedures for creating a subject authority record are demonstrated using the following example from LCSH:

**Enemy property**
Here are entered works on the treatment of enemy property taken on land. Works on enemy property taken at sea are entered under Capture at sea.

UF    Captured property
BT    Confiscations
RT    Alien property
       Requisitions, Military
       Trading with the enemy
SA    *subdivision* Confiscations and contributions *under individual wars, e.g.* World War, 1939-1945— Confiscations and contributions
NT    Booty (International law)
       Military occupation damages

1.    Code the subject heading.
       150  0    $aEnemy property

2.    Include any necessary scope notes.
       150  0    $aEnemy property
       680        $iHere are entered works on the treatment of enemy property taken on land. Works on enemy property taken at sea are entered under$aCapture at sea
       681        $iNote under$aCapture at sea

3.    Then add any general (SA) references
       150  0    $aEnemy property
       360        $isubdivision$aConfiscations and contributions$iunder individual wars, e.g. $aWorld War, 1939-1945—Confiscations and contributions
       680        $iHere are entered works on the treatment of enemy property taken on land. Works on enemy property taken at sea are entered under$aCapture at sea
       681        $iNote under$aCapture at sea

4.    Next add any "seen from" (Used For) references.

        150  0     $aEnemy property

        360       $isubdivision$aConfiscations and contributions$iunder individual wars, e.g. $aWorld War, 1939-1945—Confiscations and contributions

        450  0     $aCaptured property

        680       $iHere are entered works on the treatment of enemy property taken on land. Works on enemy property taken at sea are entered under$aCapture at sea

        681       $iNote under$aCapture at sea

5.    Then add any "seen also from" references. Note that the code "g" in subfield "w" indicates a Broader Term relationship.

        150  0     $aEnemy property

        360       $isubdivision$aConfiscations and contributions$iunder individual wars, e.g. $aWorld War, 1939-1945—Confiscations and contributions

        450  0     $aCaptured property

        550  0     $wg$aConfiscations

        680       $iHere are entered works on the treatment of enemy property taken on land. Works on enemy property taken at sea are entered under$aCapture at sea

        681       $iNote under$aCapture at sea

6.    Add related terms (only add related terms if your library has used those headings)

        150  0     $aEnemy property

        450  0     $aCaptured property

        550  0     $wg$aConfiscations

        550  0     $aAlien property

        550  0     $aRequisitions, Military

        550  0     $aTrading with the enemy

7.    Finally, include a reference(s) to a narrower term(s). Code "h" in subfield "w" indicates the Narrower Term relationship.

        150  0     $aEnemy property

        450  0     $aCaptured property

        550  0     $wg$aConfiscations

        550  0     $aAlien property

        550  0     $aRequisitions, Military

        550  0     $aTrading with the enemy

        550  0     $wh$aBooty (International law)

        550  0     $wh$aMilitary occupational damages

The final record is:

| | | |
|---|---|---|
| 150 | 0 | $aEnemy property |
| 360 | | $isubdivision$aConfiscations and contributions$iunder individual wars, e.g. $aWorld War, 1939-1945—Confiscations and contributions |
| 450 | 0 | $aCaptured property |
| 550 | 0 | $wg$aConfiscations |
| 550 | 0 | $aAlien property |
| 550 | 0 | $aRequisitions, Military |
| 550 | 0 | $aTrading with the enemy |
| 550 | 0 | $wh$aBooty (International law) |
| 550 | 0 | $wh$aMilitary occupational damages |
| 680 | | $iHere are entered works on the treatment of enemy property taken on land. Works on enemy property taken at sea are entered under$aCapture at sea |
| 681 | | $iNote under$aCapture at sea |

8.  Depending on your online system, you may have to go into each of the headings referred to, in order to establish the corresponding reciprocal references.

| | | |
|---|---|---|
| 150 | 0 | $aConfiscations |
| 550 | 0 | $wh$aBooty (International law) |
| 550 | 0 | $wh$aEnemy property |
| 550 | 0 | $wh$aMonetary gold confiscation |
| 550 | 0 | $wh$aRefugee property |
| 550 | 0 | $wh$aRequisitions, Military |

| | | |
|---|---|---|
| 150 | 0 | $aAlien property |
| 450 | 0 | $aAssets, Foreign |
| 450 | 0 | $aProperty, alien |
| 550 | 0 | $wg$aAliens |
| 550 | 0 | $wg$aInternational law |
| 550 | 0 | $aEnemy property |
| 550 | 0 | $wh$aAmerican property |
| 550 | 0 | $wh$aAustrian property |
| 550 | 0 | $wh$aBelgian property |

(and so on, as well as for other related terms)

| | | |
|---|---|---|
| 150 | 0 | $aBooty (International law) |
| 450 | 0 | $aCaptured property |
| 550 | 0 | $wg$aConfiscations |
| 550 | 0 | $wg$aEnemy property |
| 550 | 0 | $wg$aMilitary occupation |
| 550 | 0 | $wg$aPrizes |
| 550 | 0 | $wg$aSearches and seizures |

(and so on, as well as for other narrower terms)

## EXERCISE 11.1

*Using LCSH, create the necessary subject authority record for the heading **Work**, and indicate what changes need to be made to existing records.*

**Work**

Here are entered works on the physical or mental exertion of individuals to produce or accomplish something. Works on the collective human activities involved in the production and distribution of goods and services are entered under Labor.

UF   Industry (Psychology)
         Method of work
         Work, method of
BT   Human behavior
RT   Labor
         Occupations
         Work-life balance
NT   Chores
         Hours of labor
         Labor time

         . . .

# CHAPTER TWELVE
## More Practice

**EXERCISE 12.1**

*Using LCSH, find subject headings, with subdivisions where appropriate, and code using MARC 21.*

|  | Topic | Subject heading |
|---|---|---|
| 1. | AACRII—a computer based training package | |
| 2. | Adopted children : a new look at their civil rights | |
| 3. | The anti-vivisection movement : a history | |
| 4. | The art of growing daffodils | |
| 5. | The artists of Spain : works on exhibition | |
| 6. | Business English : how to write business letters | |
| 7. | Car pools in San Francisco | |
| 8. | Carrying out public relations for the Library of Congress | |
| 9. | Adolescent health services in Denmark | |
| 10. | Collected biographies of Mexican musicians | |
| 11. | Constitutional law in Maine | |
| 12. | Cooking Egyptian cuisine | |
| 13. | Cooking in Egypt | |
| 14. | Diagnosing brain abscesses | |
| 15. | A bibliography of education for librarianship | |

### EXERCISE 12.2

*Using LCSH, find subject headings, with subdivisions where appropriate, and code using MARC 21.*

| Topic | Subject heading |
|---|---|
| 1. The effects of pollution on rice-growing | |
| 2. Electric power development | |
| 3. Encyclopaedia of the Aztecs | |
| 4. Eroticism in art | |
| 5. Personal stories of American soldiers in the Korean War | |
| 6. Biological treatment of sewage | |
| 7. Grist for the mill : the flour mills of Brazil | |
| 8. Hallelujah I'm a bum: a study of tramps and hoboes | |
| 9. Harrap German-Spanish-German dictionary | |
| 10. A history of the People's Republic of China 1950-1975 | |
| 11. House plans by architects | |
| 12. How real is telekinesis? | |
| 13. How to tune a French horn | |
| 14. How to tune a piano | |
| 15. An introduction to Eskimo folksongs | |

## EXERCISE 12.3

*Using LCSH, find subject headings, with subdivisions where appropriate, and code using MARC 21.*

| Topic | Subject heading |
|---|---|
| 1. Medieval history | |
| 2. Telephone directory of Columbus, Nebraska | |
| 3. Mendicants : a history of begging | |
| 4. The model ship catalog | |
| 5. Negotiation in the hostage situation | |
| 6. A new bibliography of fiction about dogs | |
| 7. The dating of porcelain from China | |
| 8. The psychological effects of being unemployed | |
| 9. Relations between Judaism and Islam | |
| 10. Rhymes and poetry for children | |
| 11. Corrosion of iron and concrete | |
| 12. The story of the Holy Grail | |
| 13. Snakes of Kentucky | |
| 14. A study of parents without partners | |
| 15. Surfboard riding in Hawaii | |

## EXERCISE 12.4

*Using LCSH, find subject headings, with subdivisions where appropriate, and code using MARC 21.*

| Topic | Subject heading |
|---|---|
| 1. Surgeons in the Argentine Navy (Hint: check a name authority file for the Navy) | |
| 2. Pilot Creek in Texas | |
| 3. Public access to the Internet in libraries | |
| 4. Techniques for photographing birds | |
| 5. A collection of photographs of the Vietnam War (not a book of reproduced photos) | |
| 6. Television repair manual | |
| 7. Public library services to preschoolers | |
| 8. Easy dried flower pictures | |
| 9. Measuring the earth's gravitational pull | |
| 10. The five commandments of Buddhism | |
| 11. Judging English riding | |
| 12. Transportation of nuclear waste: legal requirements in Germany | |
| 13. Ice-climbing in Nepal | |
| 14. When your partner dies | |
| 15. Reusing your wastepaper | |

# ANSWERS

Note: These answers have been verified in the 37th edition of LCSH and the *Subject headings manual* current at 2015. Some answers may vary according to the editions and updates used.

## EXERCISE 1.1

1.　Subject: the theme of a work
　　Subject heading: a term (word or phrase) that represents the theme of a work

2.　There are any number of subject headings lists, including:
　　Library of Congress Subject Headings
　　Sears List of Subject Headings
　　MeSH: Medical Subject Headings
　　SCIS Subject Headings List
　　ERIC Thesaurus
　　Getty Art & Architecture Thesaurus
　　APAIS Thesaurus, etc.

## EXERCISE 1.2

*What needs do the following users have of a subject headings list?*
1.　Cataloger:
　　　Uses headings in subject cataloging
　　　Consistency maintained within catalog
2.　Reference advisor:
　　　Needs headings to construct searches when searching the catalog
3.　Library user:
　　　Needs headings to construct searches in the catalog
4.　Acquisitions officer:
　　　Uses headings to identify subject areas a library might collect in
　　　Able to search a number of sources for items
5.　Interlibrary loans officer:
　　　Uses headings to help find/verify items for loan
6.　Author:
　　　Helps author to use standard or preferred terminology

## EXERCISE 1.4

*Provide two possible meanings for each of the following terms:*

| 1. | slack | 1. | loose |
|---|---|---|---|
| | | 2. | careless |
| 2. | slam | 1. | shut with force and noise |
| | | 2. | win all tricks (cards) in one deal |
| 3. | toast | 1. | bread in slices browned on both sides by heat |
| | | 2. | words of congratulations or appreciation spoken before drinking |

| 4. | lag | 1. | fall behind |
| | | 2. | cover pipes |
| 5. | cuff | 1. | trimming on a sleeve |
| | | 2. | to strike with open hand |

## EXERCISE 1.5

*Provide synonyms for the following words or phrases:*

| 1. | author | writer |
| 2. | stamp collecting | philately |
| 3. | car | automobile, motor car |
| 4. | monograph | book |
| 5. | trailer | campervan |
| 6. | serial | journal, periodical |
| 7. | hiking | tramping |
| 8. | saturated | soaked |
| 9. | slack | loose, careless |
| 10. | corpulence | bulkiness, obesity |
| 11. | elevators | lifts |
| 12. | hirsute | hairy |
| 13. | shore | beach |
| 14. | rage | anger |
| 15. | hemp | marijuana |

## EXERCISE 1.6

*List examples of systems that use:*
1.    Controlled vocabulary:
          Many library catalogs use subject headings schemes like LCSH, SCIS, Sears etc.
          Medline, ERIC and other bibliographic databases use specialist subject thesauri
      Uncontrolled vocabulary:
          Full-text databases
          Google and similar search engines

2. *What are the advantages and disadvantages of controlled and uncontrolled vocabulary?*
      Controlled vocabulary
          Advantages
          • only one term per concept
          • records hierarchical and associative relations of a concept
          • establishes scope of each topic
          • increases probability that the same term will be used by different catalogs
          • speeds retrieval
          Disadvantages
          • highly structured
          • sometimes slow to introduce new terms or adapt to changing terminology

- may be cumbersome to use
- user must 'learn' the language

Uncontrolled vocabulary
  Advantages
  - effort and cost of indexing are reduced
  - process can be automated
  - user can use terms and synonyms requiring no additional knowledge

  Disadvantages
  - can reduce retrieved list unless all synonyms are used
  - may retrieve false hits—e.g., with homonyms

## EXERCISE 2.1

1.    d.  contain useful or important information that people normally wouldn't see
2.    c.  not eating properly and not getting enough exercise
      b.  bad features of living in towns
      c.  make resolutions to lead a healthier life
      b.  it is better to become a Buddhist
      a.  their way of life involved both exercise and relaxation

*Keywords:* lifestyle, fitness, relaxation, yoga, exercise
*Summary:* Because of our unhealthy lifestyle, we need to learn to relax, and yoga and exercise can help.

## EXERCISE 3.1

1.    'Craftsmen' is not used. 'Artisans' is the preferred term that is used.
2.    'Apprentices' is narrower than 'Artisans'.
3.    'Skilled labor' is broader than 'Artisans'.
4.    'Artisans' and 'Cottage industries'are related terms. Both are used.
5.    No.

## EXERCISE 3.2

|     | Subject heading | Correct heading |
| --- | --- | --- |
| 1. | Felix the Cat | Felix the Cat (Fictitious character) |
| 2. | Guitar—Construction | Correct |
| 3. | Fusion reactors—Fuels | Thermonuclear fuels |
| 4. | Fusion reactors—Germany | Fusion reactors |
| 5. | Semi-conductors | Semiconductors |
| 6. | Guitar and harp music | Correct |
| 7. | Heliophobus plants | Shade-tolerant plants |
| 8. | Seychelles—Coup d'etat, 1977 | Seychelles—History—Coup d'etat, 1977 |
| 9. | Coups d'etat—Seychelles | Correct |
| 10. | Tempo | TEMPO (Computer program language) OR Tempo (Music) OR Tempo (Phonetics) |

## EXERCISE 3.3

1.    Beverage industry
      Beverage processing plants

2.    Beverage industry—Employees
      Beverage industry—Employees—Labor unions
      Beverage industry—Equipment and supplies
      Beverage processing plants—Equipment and supplies

3.    Beverage industry—Canada
      Beverage industry—Canada—Employees
      Beverage industry—Employees—Labor unions—Canada
      Beverage industry—Canada—Equipment and supplies
      Beverage processing plants—Canada
      Beverage processing plants—Canada—Equipment and supplies

## EXERCISE 4.2

*Locate the following subject headings in Classification Web, and find LCC and DDC correlations for them.*

1. Dogs—Judging        LCC:  SF425.2
                       DDC:  636.70811 (2 uses)
                             636.710973 (1 use)

2. Politics and culture    LCC:  JA75.7 (41 uses)
                                 HM621 (5 uses)
                                 HM101 (3 uses) and so on
                          DDC:  306.2 (20 uses)
                                305 (4 uses)
                                303.4833 (1 use)
                                306.201 (1 use)

3. Rice                 LCC:  SB191.R5 (43 uses)
                              TX558.R5 (5 uses)
                              HD9066.A2 (3 uses) and so on
                       DDC:  633.18 (10 uses)
                             338.17318 (2 uses)
                             633.18095 (1 use) and so on

*Using the Bibliographic Correlation database, find a subject heading for the following LCC numbers:*

4. BL290                Soul

5. UG734.A98            Air defenses—Azerbaijan

6. PS3511.A9327         Large type books

*Using the Bibliographic Correlation database, find a subject heading for the following DDC numbers:*

7. 599.539             Porpoises

8. 647.944             Hotels—Europe—Directories
                       *(plus many other variations, including Pets and travel—France (!))*

9. 636.8089100222      Cats—Anatomy—Atlases

## EXERCISE 4.3

| Topic | Subject heading |
|---|---|
| 1. Cooking with rice | Cooking—Rice |
| 2. Rock lobsters | Spiny lobsters |
| 3. Conflicts of interest | Conflict of interests |
| 4. Low sodium diet | Salt-free diet |
| 5. Stained glass | Glass painting and staining |
| 6. Supervision of spiritual directors | Spiritual directors—Supervision of |
| 7. Tibetan gilt bronzes | Gilt bronzes, Tibetan |
| 8. Women heroes on television | Women heroes on television |
| 9. Toybraries | Toy lending libraries |
| 10. Carbon content of plant biomass | Plant biomass—Carbon content |

## EXERCISE 5.1

| Topic | Subject heading |
|---|---|
| 1. The sea | Ocean |
| 2. Adoption services | Adoption agencies |
| 3. Adriatic Islands | Islands of the Adriatic |
| 4. Children as actors | Child actors |
| 5. Ways of monitoring fetal heart rate | Fetal heart rate monitoring |
| 6. The impact of highway traffic noise | Traffc noise |
| 7. Oceanic drilling ships in the Atlantic | Deep-sea drilling ships—Atlantic Ocean |
| 8. Catalan political satire | Political satire, Catalan |
| 9. An introduction to prehistoric agriculture | Agriculture, Prehistoric |
| 10. The wonders of horseradish | Horse-radish |

## EXERCISE 5.2

| Topic | Subject heading |
|---|---|
| 1. Morris West's slide collections | West, Morris L., 1916-1999 — Slide collections *(as per SA note under Slides (Photography) —Private collections)* |
| 2. Water conservation and irrigation efficiency | 1. Water conservation<br>2. Irrigation efficiency |
| 3. Cartoon-makers | Animators |
| 4. Electric condensers | Capacitors |
| 5. Music for organ and flute | Flute and organ music |
| 6. Sulky racing | Harness racing |

| | | |
|---|---|---|
| 7. | Harmony on the keyboard | Keyboard harmony |
| 8. | Prehistoric cartography | Cartography, Prehistoric |
| 9. | The benefits of asparaginic acid | Aspartic acid |
| 10. | Bakery products | Baked products |

## EXERCISE 7.1

| | Topic | Subject heading |
|---|---|---|
| 1. | The cost of constructing railroads | Railroads—Design and construction—Costs<br>650 #0$aRailroads$xDesign and construction$xCosts. |
| 2. | Extensions to buildings | Buildings—Additions<br>650 #0$aBuildings$xAdditions. |
| 3. | Synthesis in organic chemistry | Organic compounds—Synthesis<br>650 #0$aOrganic compounds$xSynthesis. |
| 4. | Data processing in credit bureaus | Credit bureaus—Data processing<br>650 #0$aCredit bureaus$xData processing. |
| 5. | The rights and wages of employees in credit unions | 1. Credit unions—Employees<br>2. Wages—Credit unions<br>3. Employee rights<br><br>650 #0$aCredit unions$xEmployees.<br>650 #0$aWages$xCredit unions.<br>650 #0$aEmployee rights. |
| 6. | John Brown's raid on Harpers Ferry | Harpers Ferry (W.Va.)—History—John Brown's Raid, 1859<br>651 #0$aHarpers Ferry (W.Va)$vHistory$yJohn Brown's Raid, 1859. |
| 7. | The 1929 depression in Chicago | Depressions—1929—Illinois—Chicago<br>650 #0$aDepressions$y1929$zIllinois$zChicago. |
| 8. | The diagnosis of unipolar depression | Depression, Mental—Diagnosis<br>650 #0$aDepression, Mental$xDiagnosis. |
| 9. | Renaissance engraving | Engraving, Renaissance<br>650 #0$aEngraving, Renaissance. |
| 10. | Hunting with bows and arrows | Bowhunting<br>650 #0$aBowhunting. |

## EXERCISE 7.2

Banks and banking—China
Banks and banking—Automation
Banks and banking—China—Automation
Banks and banking—Automation—Equipment and supplies
Banks and banking—China—Automation—Equipment and supplies
Banks and banking—Data processing
Banks and banking—China—Data processing
Banks and banking—Data processing—Contracting out
Banks and banking—Data processing—Contracting out—China
Banks and banking—Government ownership
Banks and banking—Government ownership—China

Banks and banking—Government ownership—Law and legislation
Banks and banking—Government ownership—Law and legislation—China

## EXERCISE 7.3

| | Topic | Subject heading |
|---|---|---|
| 1. | Religious aspects of animal experiments from the Islamic viewpoint | Animal experimentation—Religious aspects—Islam 650 #0$aAnimal experimentation$xReligious aspects$xIslam. |
| 2. | Subject headings for astronomy | Subject headings—Astronomy 650 #0$aSubject headings$xAstronomy. |
| 3. | Christian beliefs about salt | Salt—Religious aspects—Christianity 650 #0$aSalt$xReligious aspects$xChristianity. |
| 4. | German words and phrases in the English language | English language—Foreign words and phrases— German 650 #0$aEnglish language$xForeign words and phrases$xGerman. |
| 5. | Jewish aspects of codependency | Codependency—Religious aspects—Judaism 650 #0$aCodependency$xReligious aspects$xJudaism. |

## EXERCISE 8.1

| | Heading | Correct/ Incorrect | Reason and correct form (if incorrect) |
|---|---|---|---|
| 1. | Dentistry—Law and legislation | Incorrect | Dental laws and legislation |
| 2. | Buildings—Maintenance | Correct | |
| 3. | Buildings—Maintenance and repair | Allowed, but... | Heading using a free-floating subdivision is allowed, but prefer Buildings— Maintenance, which is included in the list |
| 4. | Books—Reviews—Periodicals | Correct | |
| 5. | Dentistry—Book reviews | Correct | |
| 6. | Real property—Finance, Personal | Incorrect | **--Finance, Personal** is only allowed under names of individual persons, and under classes of persons and ethnic groups. You may use: 1. Real property 2. Finance, personal |
| 7. | Chicago (Ill.)—Appropriations and expenditure | Incorrect | Chicago (Ill.)—Appropriations and expenditures |
| 8. | Chamber music—Early works to 1800—England | Incorrect | Chamber music—England—Early works to 1800 |
| 9. | Paper industry—History | Correct | |
| 10. | Parachutes—Testing—Equipment—Certification—United States | Incorrect | Parachutes—Testing—Equipment and supplies—Certification—United States |

## Exercise 8.2

| | Topic | Subject heading |
|---|---|---|
| 1. | Bibliography on plant migration | Plants—Migration—Bibliography<br>650 #0$aPlants$xMigration$vBibliography. |
| 2. | Colonization of Zimbabwe | Zimbabwe—Colonization<br>651 #0$aZimbabwe$xColonization. |
| 3. | Pensions of bus drivers in Mexico | Bus drivers—Pensions—Mexico<br>650 #0$aBus drivers$xPensions$zMexico. |
| 4. | History of the laws regulating collection agencies in New Zealand | Collection agencies—Law and legislation—New Zealand—History<br>650 #0$aCollection agencies$xLaw and legislation $zNew Zealand$xHistory. |
| 5. | Satirical cartoons of nurses | Nurses—Caricatures and cartoons<br>650 #0$aNurses$vCaricatures and cartoons. |
| 6. | Laboratories for sensory evaluation in Geneva | Sensory evaluation—Switzerland— Geneva—Laboratories<br>650 #0$aSensory evaluation$zSwitzerland $zGeneva$xLaboratories. |
| 7. | Diagnosis of mouth cancer in Glasgow | Mouth—Cancer—Diagnosis—Scotland—Glasgow<br>650 #0$aMouth$xCancer$xDiagnosis$zScotland $zGlasgow. |
| 8. | Testing of instruments used in nuclear power plants in Tokyo | Nuclear power plants—Japan—Tokyo—Instruments—Testing<br>650 #0$aNuclear power plants$zJapan$zTokyo $xInstruments$xTesting. |
| 9. | Deterioration of murals in Venice | Mural painting and decoration—Deterioration—Italy— Venice<br>650 #0$aMural painting and decoration $xDeterioration $zItaly $zVenice. |
| 10. | Chinese coiffures in the 18th century | Hairstyles—China—History—18th century<br>650 #0$aHairstyles$zChina$xHistory$y18th century. |

## Exercise 8.3

| | Topic | Pattern heading | Heading |
|---|---|---|---|
| 1. | The lifecycle of the chipmunk | Fishes or Cattle | Chipmunks—Life cycles |
| 2. | Vaccinating cats | Cattle | Cats—Vaccination |
| 3. | Ellipsis in Albanian | English language | Albanian language—Ellipsis |
| 4. | The psychotropic effects of iodine | Copper | Iodine—Psychotropic effects |
| 5. | Economic conditions of Dutch colonies in Asia | Great Britain—Colonies | Netherlands—Colonies—Asia—Economic conditions |
| 6. | Breeding lions | Cattle | Lion—Breeding |
| 7. | Origins of Zen Buddhism in Japan | Buddhism | Zen Buddhism—Japan—Origin |

| 8. | Anti-lock brake systems for dune buggies | Automobiles | Dune buggies—Antilock brake systems |
| 9. | How drugs affect the brain | Foot or Heart | Brain—Effect of drugs on |
| 10. | Regional variations in the macadamia nut industry | Retail trade | Macadamia nut industry—Regional disparities |
| 11. | Production standards of films adapted from Arabic children's stories | English literature | Children's stories, Arabic—Film adaptations—Production standards |
| 12. | Research on methods of painting of plastics | Metals | Plastics—Painting—Research |
| 13. | How French has had an impact on English | English language | 1. French language—Influence on English<br><br>2. English language—Foreign elements—French |
| 14. | Genetic engineering of sheep in New Zealand | Cattle | Sheep—Genetic engineering—New Zealand |
| 15. | How to fix vapour lock problems in buses | Automobiles | Buses—Fuel systems—Vapor lock—Repairing |

## EXERCISE 8.4

| | Topic | Subject heading |
|---|---|---|
| 1. | Liver—Size | Correct |
| 2. | Canada. Parliament—Duties of members | Canada. Parliament—Powers and duties |
| 3. | Spring wheat—Diseases and pests—Italy—Biological Control | Wheat—Diseases and pests—Biological control—Italy |
| 4. | Chinese-French War, 1884-1885—Battles | Sino-French War, 1884-1885—Campaigns |
| 5. | Guitar—Strings—Materials | Guitar strings—Materials |
| 6. | Dogs—Embryos—Canada—Transplantation | Dogs—Embryos—Transplantation—Canada |
| 7. | Llamas—Peru—Handling | Llamas—Handling—Peru |
| 8. | Toes, Dislocation of | Toes—Dislocation |
| 9. | Ranunculus—Time of flowering | Ranunculus—Flowering time |
| 10. | Canola—Disease and pest resistance—Genetic aspects | Correct |

## EXERCISE 9.1

| | Topic | Subject heading |
|---|---|---|
| 1. | Kythnos Island | Kythnos Island (Greece) |
| 2. | Isle Royale National Park | Isle Royale National Park (Mich.) |
| 3 | Royal National Park (near Sydney, New South Wales, Australia) | Royal National Park (N.S.W.) |

| | | |
|---|---|---|
| 4. | Central Park (in New York) | Central Park (New York, N.Y.) |
| 5. | Statue of Liberty | Statue of Liberty (New York, N.Y.) |
| 6. | Grand Canyon | Grand Canyon (Ariz.) |
| 7. | Tower Hamlets Cemetery (London) | Tower Hamlets Cemetery Park (London, England) |
| 8. | Merri River | Merri River (Vic.) |
| 9. | London River (in France) | London River (France and Switzerland) |
| 10. | Amazon River | Amazon River |
| 11. | Death Valley | Death Valley (Calif. and Nev.) |
| 12. | St. Patrick's Street (Ireland) | Saint Patrick's Street (Cork, Ireland) |
| 13. | 17th Street in Washington | Seventeenth Street (Washington, D.C.) |
| 14. | Highway 40 (United States) | United States Highway 40 |
| 15. | Hilo Bay | Hilo Bay (Hawaii) |
| 16. | Pearl Bridge (in Japan) | Akashi Kaikyō Ōshshi (Kōbe-shi, Japan) |
| 17. | Ayers Rock National Park | Uluru-Kata Tjuta National Park (N.T.) |
| 18. | Mount Whitney in California | Whitney, Mount (Calif.) |
| 19. | The Vatican | Vatican Palace (Vatican City) |
| 20. | Wailing Wall (in Jerusalem) | Western Wall (Jerusalem) |
| 21. | Hyde Park in Sydney, Australia | Hyde Park (Sydney, N.S.W.) |

## EXERCISE 9.2

| | Topic | Subject heading |
|---|---|---|
| 1. | Diseases of the eyelids in China | Eyelids—Diseases—China<br>650 #0$aEyelids$xDiseases$zChina. |
| 2. | Diseases of the limbs in Africa | Extremities (Anatomy)—Diseases—Africa<br>650 #0$aExtremities (Anatomy)$xDiseases$zAfrica. |
| 3. | Taxation of show business personalities in Venezuela | Entertainers—Taxation—Venezuela<br>650 #0$aEntertainers$xTaxation$zVenezuela. |
| 4. | The labelling of bread in Montréal | Bread—Labeling—Québec—Montréal<br>650 #0$aBread$xLabeling$z Québec $zMontréal. |
| 5. | The legislation on bread labelling in Nova Scotia | Bread—Labeling—Law and legislation—Nova Scotia<br>650 #0$aBread$xLabeling$xLaw and legislation$zNova Scotia. |
| 6. | Abnormalities of cattle in Argentina | Cattle—Abnormalities—Argentina<br>650 #0$aCattle$xAbnormalities$zArgentina. |
| 7. | Collective agreements in the airlines in Belgium | Collective labor agreements—Aeronautics—Belgium<br>650 #0$aCollective labor agreements$xAeronautics $zBelgium. |
| 8. | Job stress in health professionals in Singapore | Medical personnel—Job stress—Singapore<br>650 #0$aMedical personnel$xJob stress$zSingapore. |

9.    A report on kumara plant pests in Bali (a province of Indonesia)

Sweet potatoes—Diseases and pests—Indonesia—Bali
650 #0$aSweet potatoes$xDiseases and pests $zIndonesia$zBali.

10.    Historical monuments in Ballarat, Victoria

Monuments—Victoria—Ballarat
650 #0$aMonuments$zVictoria$zBallarat.

## EXERCISE 9.3

| Incorrect | Correct |
|---|---|
| 1.    Artists—Beijing | Artists—China—Beijing |
| 2.    Phoenix—Telephone directories | Phoenix (Ariz.)—Telephone directories |
| 3.    Museums—Pheonix | Museums—Arizona—Phoenix |
| 4.    Peonies—Tokyo | Peonies—Japan—Tokyo |
| 5.    Hanoi—Aerial views | Hanoi (Vietnam)—Aerial views |
| 6.    Soccer—Hanoi | Soccer—Vietnam—Hanoi |
| 7.    Cairo—Economic conditions | Cairo (Egypt)—Economic conditions |
| 8.    Berlin—Statistics | Berlin (Germany)—Statistics |
| 9.    Flea markets—Mexico City - Directories | Flea markets—Mexico—Mexico City—Directories |
| 10.    Surfing—Sydney | Surfing—Australia—Sydney<br>*or if in Australia:*<br>Surfing—New South Wales—Sydney |
| 11.    Cheese—Copenhagen | Cheese—Denmark—Copenhagen |
| 12.    Toronto—Maps | Toronto (Ont.) —Maps |
| 13.    Restaurants—Toronto—Guidebooks | Restaurants—Ontario—Toronto—Guidebooks |
| 14.    Bedding—Suva | Bedding—Fiji—Suva |
| 15.    Tombs—Decoration—New Delhi | Tombs—Decoration—India—New Delhi |

## EXERCISE 9.4

| Topic | Subject heading |
|---|---|
| 1.    American libraries | Libraries—United States<br>650 #0$aLibraries$zUnited States. |
| 2.    Hospitals in Albuquerque, New Mexico, USA | Hospitals—New Mexico—Albuquerque<br>650 #0$sHospitals$zNew Mexico$zAlbuquerque. |
| 3.    A field guide to birds around Billings in Montana, USA | Birds—Montana—Billings—Identification<br>650 #0$aBirds$zMontana$zBillings$xIdentification. |
| 4.    Laws regulating online gambling in the Eastern Mediterranean | Internet gambling—Law and legislation—Middle East<br>650 #0$aInternet gambling$xLaw and legislation $zMiddle East. |
| 5.    A report on the police in Utah, USA | Police—Utah<br>650 #0$aPolice$zUtah. |
| 6.    Body surfing on the Gold Coast of Queensland (in Australia) | Surfing—Australia—Gold Coast (Qld.)<br>650 #0$aSurfing$zAustralia$zGold Coast (Qld.) |

*Or if cataloging in Australia:*
Surfing—Queensland—Gold Coast
650 #0$aSurfing$zQueensland$zGold Coast.

7.  Black colleges in the United States

African American universities and colleges
650 #0$aAfrican American universities and colleges.

8.  Australian badgers (Vombatidae) of the south-eastern region of Australia

Wombats—Australia, Southeastern
650 #0$aWombats$zAustralia, Southeastern.

9.  Art colonies in Banff, Canada

Artist colonies—Alberta—Banff
650 #0$aArtist colonies$zAlberta$zBanff.

10. Art colonies in Kuala Lumpor, Malaysia

Artist colonies—Malaysia—Kuala Lumpor
650 #0$aArtist colonies$zMalaysia$zKuala Lumpor.

11. Traditional Spanish folk beliefs

Folklore—Spain
650 #0$aFolklore$zSpain.

12. Painters from Rocksprings, Wyoming, USA

Painters—Wyoming—Rocksprings
650 #0$aPainters$zWyoming$zRocksprings.

13. Research into the climate of Darwin, NT (in Australia)

Climatology—Research—Australia—Darwin (N.T.)
650 #0$aClimatology$xResearch$zAustralia$zDarwin (N.T.)

*Or if cataloging in Australia:*
Climatology—Research—Northern Territory–Darwin
650 #0$aClimatology$xResearch$zNorthern Territory $z Darwin

14. Bridges in Rome (in Italy)

Bridges—Italy—Rome
650 #0$aBridges$zItaly$zRome.

15. Walking in Cardiff (in Britain)

Walking—Wales—Cardiff
650 #0$aWalking$zWales$zCardiff.

## EXERCISE 10.1

| Topic | Subject heading |
|---|---|
| 1. Shakespeare | Shakespeare, William, 1564-1616<br>600 10$aShakespeare, William,$d1564-1616. |
| 2. Antonia Byatt | Byatt, A. S. (Antonia Susan), 1936–<br>600 10$aByatt, A. S.$q(Antonia Susan),$d1936– |
| 3. T.S. Eliot | Eliot, T.S. (Thomas Stearns), 1888-1965<br>600 10$aEliot, T. S.$q(Thomas Stearns),$d1888-1963. |
| 4. Joan of Arc | Joan, of Arc, Saint, 1412-1431<br>600 00$aJoan,$cof Arc, Saint,$d1412-1431. |
| 5. Queen Elizabeth II | Elizabeth II, Queen of Great Britain, 1926–<br>600 00$aElizabeth$bII,$cQueen of Great Britain,$d1926– |
| 6. The Tower of London | Tower of London (London, England)<br>610 20$aTower of London (London, England) |
| 7. Empire State Building | Empire State Building (New York, N.Y.)<br>610 20$aEmpire State Building (New York, N.Y.) |

| | | |
|---|---|---|
| 8. | Augustus Agar | Agar, Augustus, 1890-1968<br>600 10$aAgar, Augustus,$d1890-1968. |
| 9. | The Tyree Family | Tyree family<br>600 30$aTyree family. |
| 10. | Immanuel Kant | Kant, Immanuel, 1724-1804<br>600 10$aKant, Immanuel,$d1724-1804. |

## EXERCISE 10.2

| | Topic | Subject heading |
|---|---|---|
| 1. | Biography of Earl Warren, a governor of California | 1. Warren, Earl, 1891-1974<br>2. Governors—California—Biography |
| 2. | Biography of American singer Tony Bennett | 1. Bennett, Tony, 1926–<br>2. Singers—United States—Biography |
| 3. | A collective biography of the last 10 Prime Ministers of Canada and the events that took place during their tenure | 1. Prime Ministers—Canada—Biography |
| 4. | The history of the Pulitzer Prize | 1. Pulitzer Prizes—History |
| 5. | The history of the Taylor family | 1. Taylor family |
| 6. | Biography of Lachlan Macquarie, a governor of New South Wales | 1. Macquarie, Lachlan, 1761-1824<br>2. Governors—Australia—New South Wales—Biography.<br>*or if in Australia:*<br>2. Governors—New South Wales—Biography. |
| 7. | Biography of the Australian writer Patrick White | 1. White, Patrick, 1912-1990<br>2. Authors, Australian—20$^{th}$ century—Biography  *or*<br>2. Novelists, Australian—20$^{th}$ century—Biography |

## EXERCISE 11.1

*New records:*
150  0  $aWork
450  0  $aIndustry (Psychology)
450  0  $aMethod of work
450  0  $aWork, Method of
550  0  $wg$aHuman behavior
550  0  $aLabor
550  0  $aOccupations
550  0  $aWork-life balance
550  0  $wh$aChores
550  0  $wh$aHours of labor
550  0  $wh$aLabor time
680  0  $iHere are entered works on the physical or mental exertion of individuals to produce or accomplish something. Works on the collective human activities involved in the production and distribution of goods and services are entered under Labor.

*Changes:*

150  0  $aHuman behavior
550  0  $wh$aWork

150  0  $aLabor
550  0  $aWork

150  0  $aOccupations
550  0  $aWork

150  0  $aWork-life balance
550  0  $aWork

150  0  $aChores
550  0  $wg$aWork

150  0  $aHours of labor
550  0  $wg$aWork

150  0  $aLabor time
550  0  $wg$aWork

## EXERCISE 12.1

| Topic | Subject heading |
|---|---|
| 1. AACRII—a computer-based training package | 1. Anglo-American cataloguing rules—Computer assisted instruction<br>2. Descriptive cataloging—Rules<br>630 00$a Anglo-American cataloguing rules$xComputer assisted instruction.<br>650 #0$aDescriptive cataloguing$xRules. |
| 2. Adopted children : a new look at their civil rights | Adopted children—Civil rights<br>650 #0$aAdopted children$xCivil rights. |
| 3. The anti-vivisection movement : a history | Vivisection—History<br>650 #0$aVivisection$xHistory. |
| 4. The art of growing daffodils | Daffodils<br>650 #0$aDaffodils. |
| 5. The artists of Spain : works on exhibition | Artists—Spain<br>650 #0$aArtists$zSpain. |
| 6. Business English : how to write business letters | 1. English language—Business English<br>2. Commercial correspondence<br>650 #0$aEnglish language$xBusiness English.<br>650 #0$aCommercial correspondence. |
| 7. Car pools in San Francisco | Car pools—California—San Francisco<br>650 #0$aCar pools$zCalifornia$zSan Francisco. |
| 8. Carrying out public relations for the Library of Congress | Library of Congress—Public relations<br>610 20$aLibrary of Congress$xPublic relations. |
| 9. Adolescent health services in Denmark | Teenagers—Medical care—Denmark<br>650 #0$aTeenagers$xMedical care$zDenmark. |

| | | |
|---|---|---|
| 10. | Collected biographies of Mexican musicians | Musicians—Mexico—Biography<br>650 #0$aMusicians$zMexico$vBiography. |
| 11. | Constitutional law in maine | Constitutional law—Maine<br>650 #0$aConstitutional law$zMaine. |
| 12. | Cooking Egyptian cuisine | Cooking, Egyptian<br>650 #0$aCooking, Egyptian. |
| 13. | Cooking in Egypt | Cooking—Egypt<br>650 #0$aCooking$zEgypt. |
| 14. | Diagnosing brain abscesses | Brain—Abscess<br>650 #0$aBrain$xAbscess. |
| 15. | A bibliography of education for librarianship | Library education—Bibliography<br>650 #0$aLibrary education$vBibliography. |

## EXERCISE 12.2

| | Topic | Subject heading |
|---|---|---|
| 1. | The effects of pollution on rice-growing | Rice—Effect of pollution on<br>650 #0$aRice$xEffect of pollution on. |
| 2. | Electric power development | Electrification<br>650 #0$aElectrification. |
| 3. | Encyclopaedia of the Aztecs | Aztecs—Encyclopedias<br>650 #0$aAztecs$vEncyclopedias. |
| 4. | Eroticism in art | Erotic art<br>650 #0$aErotic art. |
| 5. | Personal stories of American soldiers in the Korean War | Korean War, 1950-1953—Personal narratives, American<br>650 #0$aKorean War, 1950-1953$vPersonal narratives, American. |
| 6. | Biological treatment of sewage | Sewage—Purification—Biological treatment<br>650 #0$aSewage$xPurification$xBiological treatment. |
| 7. | Grist for the mill: the flour mills of Brazil | Flour mills—Brazil<br>650 #0$aFlour mills$zBrazil. |
| 8. | Hallelujah I'm a bum: a study of tramps and hoboes | Tramps<br>650 #0$aTramps. |
| 9. | Harrap German-Spanish-German dictionary | 1. German language—Dictionaries— Spanish<br>2. Spanish language—Dictionaries— German<br>650 #0$aGerman language$vDictionaries$xSpanish.<br>650 #0$aSpanish language$vDictionaries$xGerman. |
| 10. | A history of the People's Republic of China 1950-1975 | China—History—1949-1976<br>650 #0$aChina$xHistory$y1949-1976. |
| 11. | House plans by architects | Architecture, Domestic— Designs and plans<br>650 #0$aArchitecture, Domestic$vDesigns and plans. |
| 12. | How real is telekinesis? | Psychokinesis<br>650 #0$aPsychokinesis. |
| 13. | How to tune a French horn | Horn (Musical instrument) —Tuning |

650 #0$aHorn (Musical instrument)$xTuning.

14.    How to tune a piano

Piano—Tuning
650 #0$aPiano$xTuning.

15.    An introduction to Eskimo folksongs

Folk songs, Eskimo
650 #0$aFolk songs, Eskimo.

## Exercise 12.3

| Topic | Subject heading |
| --- | --- |
| 1. Medieval history | Middle Ages<br>650 #0$aMiddle Ages. |
| 2. Telephone directory of Columbus, Nebraska | Columbus (Nebr.)—Telephone directories<br>651 #0$aColumbus (Nebr.)$vTelephone directories. |
| 3. Mendicants: a history of begging | 1. Beggars—History<br>2. Begging—History<br>650 #0$aBeggars$xHistory.<br>650 #0$aBegging$xHistory. |
| 4. The model ship catalog | Ship models—Catalogs<br>650 #0$aShip models$vCatalogs. |
| 5. Negotiation in the hostage situation | Hostage negotiations<br>650 #0$aHostage negotiations. |
| 6. A new bibliography of fiction about dogs | Dogs—Fiction—Bibliography<br>650 #0$aDogs$vFiction$vBibliography. |
| 7. The dating of porcelain from China | Porcelain—China—Dating<br>650 #0$aPorcelain$zChina$xDating. |
| 8. The psychological effects of being unemployed | Unemployment—Psychological aspects<br>650 #0$aUnemployment$xPsychological aspects. |
| 9. Relations between Judaism and Islam | 1. Judaism— Relations—Islam<br>2. Islam—Relations—Judaism<br>650 #0$aJudaism$xRelations$xIslam.<br>650 #0$aIslam$xRelations$xJudaism. |
| 10. Rhymes and poetry for children | Children's poetry<br>650 #0$aChildren's poetry. |
| 11. Corrosion of iron and concrete | 1. Iron—Corrosion<br>2. Concrete—Corrosion<br>650 #0$aIron$xCorrosion.<br>650 #0$aConcrete$xCorrosion. |
| 12. The story of the Holy Grail | Grail<br>650 #0$aGrail. |
| 13. Snakes of Kentucky | Snakes—Kentucky<br>650 #0$aSnakes$zKentucky. |
| 14. A study of parents without partners | Single parents<br>650 #0$aSingle parents. |
| 15. Surfboard riding in Hawaii | Surfing—Hawaii<br>650 #0$aSurfing$zHawaii. |

## EXERCISE 12.4

| Topic | Subject heading |
|---|---|
| 1. Surgeons in the Argentine Navy (check a name authority file for the Navy) | Argentina. Armada—Surgeons<br>610 10$aArgentina. Armada$xSurgeons. |
| 2. Pilot Creek in Texas | Pilot Grove Creek (Tex.)<br>651 #0$aPilot Grove Creek (Tex.) |
| 3. Public access to the Internet in libraries | Internet access for library users<br>650 #0$aInternet access for library users. |
| 4. Techniques for photographing birds | Photography of birds<br>650 #0$aPhotography of birds. |
| 5. A collection of photographs of the Vietnam War (not a book of reproduced photos) | Vietnam War, 1961-1975—Photographs<br>650 #0$aVietnam War, 1961-1975$vPhotographs. |
| 6. Television repair manual | Television—Repairing—Handbooks, manuals, etc.<br>650 #0$aTelevision$xRepairing$vHandbooks, manuals, etc. |
| 7. Public library services to preschoolers | Libraries and preschool children<br>650 #0$aLibraries and preschool children. |
| 8. Easy dried flower pictures | Preserved flower pictures<br>650 #0$aPreserved flower pictures. |
| 9. Measuring the earth's gravitational pull | Gravity—Measurement<br>650 #0$aGravity$xMeasurement. |
| 10. The five commandments of Buddhism | Five Precepts (Buddhism)<br>650 #0$aFive Precepts (Buddhism) |
| 11. Judging English horse riding | Horsemanship—Officiating<br>650 #0$aHorsemanship$xOfficiating. |
| 12. Transportation of nuclear wastes: legal requirements in Germany | Radioactive wastes—Transportation—Law and legislation—Germany<br>650 #0$aRadioactive wastes$xTransportation$xLaw and legislation$zGermany. |
| 13. Ice-climbing in Nepal | Snow and ice climbing—Nepal<br>650 #0$aSnow and ice climbing$zNepal. |
| 14. When your partner dies | 1. Widowhood<br>2. Bereavement<br>650 #0$aWidowhood.<br>650 #0$aBereavement. |
| 15. Reusing your wastepaper | Waste paper—Recycling<br>650 #0$aWaste paper$xRecycling. |

# Free-Floating Subdivisions (H 1095)

## Form and Topical Subdivisions of General Application

Scope notes explaining the use of individual subdivisions are given in H 1095 of the *Manual*. Form subdivisions are underlined in the list below.

—Abbreviations

—Abbreviations—Dictionaries

—Abbreviations of titles

—Ability testing *(May Subd Geog)*

—Abstracting and indexing *(May Subd Geog)*

—Abstracts

—Access control *(May Subd Geog)*

—Accidents *(May Subd Geog)*

—Accidents—Investigation *(May Subd Geog)*

—Accounting

—Accreditation *(May Subd Geog)*

—Acronyms

—Acronyms—Dictionaries

—Administration

—Aerial photographs

—Air conditioning *(May Subd Geog)*

—Air conditioning—Control *(May Subd Geog)*

—Amateurs' manuals

—Analysis

—Anecdotes

—Anniversaries, etc.

—Archival resources

—Archives

—Archives—Microform catalogs

—Art

—Atlases

—Audio-visual aids

—Audio-visual aids—Catalogs

—Audiocasette catalogs

—Audiotape catalogs

—Auditing

—Authorship

—Authorship—Style manuals

—Automatic control

—Automation

—Autonomous communities

—Autonomous regions

—Awards *(May Subd Geog)*

—Barrier-free design *(May Subd Geog)*

—Biblical teaching

—Bibliography

—Bibliography—Catalogs

—Bibliography—Early

—Bibliography—Exhibitions

—Bibliography—Methodology

—Bibliography—Microform catalogs

—Bibliography—Union lists

—Bibliography of bibliographies

—Bio-bibliography

—Bio-bibliography—Dictionaries

—Biography

—Biography—Dictionaries

—Biography—Dictionaries—French, [Italian, etc.]

—Biography—History and criticism

—Blogs

—Book reviews

—Buildings

—By-laws

—By-products

—Calendars

—Calibration *(May Subd Geog)*

—Cantons

—Caricatures and cartoons

—Case studies

—Catalogs

—Catalogs and collections *(May Subd Geog)*

—CD-ROM catalogs

—Censorship  *(May Subd Geog)*

—Centennial celebrations, etc.

—Certification  *(May Subd Geog)*

—Charitable contributions  *(May Subd Geog)*

—Charts, diagrams, etc.

—Chronology

—Circulation

—Citizen participation

—Classification

—Cleaning  *(May Subd Geog)*

—Code numbers

—Code words

—Cold weather conditions

—Collectibles  *(May Subd Geog)*

—Collection and preservation  *(May Subd Geog)*

—Collectors and collecting  *(May Subd Geog)*

—Colonies

—Comic books, strips, etc.

—Communication systems

—Compact disc catalogs

—Comparative method

—Comparative studies

—Competitions  *(May Subd Geog)*

—Composition

—Computer-aided design  *(May Subd Geog)*

—Computer-assisted instruction

—Computer games

—Computer network resources

—Computer networks  *(May Subd Geog)*

—Computer networks—Security measures  *(May Subd Geog)*

—Computer programs

—Computer simulation

—Concordances

—Congresses

—Congresses—Attendance

—Conservation and restoration  *(May Subd Geog)*

—Control  *(May Subd Geog)*

—Conversion tables

—Cooling  *(May Subd Geog)*

—Corrosion  *(May Subd Geog)*

—Corrupt practices  *(May Subd Geog)*

—Cost control

—Cost effectiveness

—Cost of operation

—Costs

—Cross-cultural studies

—Cult  *(May Subd Geog)*

—Curricula  *(May Subd Geog)*

—Customer services  *(May Subd Geog)*

—Data processing

—Data tape catalogs

—Databases

—Dating

—Decision making

—Defects  *(May Subd Geog)*

—Defects—Reporting  *(May Subd Geog)*

—Defense measures  *(May Subd Geog)*

—Departments

—Design

—Design and construction

—Design and plans

—Deterioration

—Dictionaries

—Dictionaries—French, [Italian. etc.]

—Dictionaries—Polyglot

—Dictionaries, Juvenile

—Digitization  *(May Subd Geog)*

—Directories

—Discipline

—Discography

—Documentation  *(May Subd Geog)*

—Drama

—Drawings

—Drying  *(May Subd Geog)*

—Dust control  *(May Subd Geog)*

—Early works to 1800

—Earthquake effects  *(May Subd Geog)*

—Econometric models

—Economic aspects  *(May Subd Geog)*

—Electromechanical analogies

—<u>Electronic discussion groups</u>
—Electronic information resources
—Employees
—<u>Encyclopedias</u>
—<u>Encyclopedias, Juvenile</u>
—Endowments
—Energy conservation *(May Subd Geog)*
—Energy consumption *(May Subd Geog)*
—Environmental aspects *(May Subd Geog)*
—Equipment and supplies
—Estimates *(May Subd Geog)*
—Evaluation
—Examinations
—Examinations—Study guides
—<u>Examination, questions, etc.</u>
—<u>Excerpts</u>
—<u>Exhibitions</u>
—Experiments
—Expertising *(May Subd Geog)*
—<u>Facsimiles</u>
—<u>Fiction</u>
—Fieldwork *(May Subd Geog)*
—<u>Film catalogs</u>
—Finance
—Fires and fire prevention *(May Subd Geog)*
—<u>Folklore</u>
—Food service *(May Subd Geog)*
—Forecasting
—Foreign countries
—Foreign influences
—Forgeries *(May Subd Geog)*
—<u>Forms</u>
—<u>Formulae, receipts, prescriptions</u>
—Fuel systems
—Fume control *(May Subd Geog)*
—Geographic information systems *(May Subd Geog)*
—Government policy *(May Subd Geog)*
—Grading *(May Subd Geog)*
—Graphic methods
—<u>Guidebooks</u>

—<u>Handbooks, manuals, etc.</u>
—Health aspects *(May Subd Geog)*
—Heating and ventilation *(May Subd Geog)*
—Heating and ventilation—Control *(May Subd Geog)*
—Heraldry
—Historiography
—History
—History—To 1500
—History—16th century
—History—17th century
—History—18th century
—History—19th century
—History—20th century
—History—21st century
—History—Chronology
—History—Philosophy
—History—Sources
—History and criticism
—History of doctrines
—History of doctrines—Early church, ca. 30-600
—History of doctrines—Middle Ages, 600-1500
—History of doctrines—16th century
—History of doctrines—17th century
—History of doctrines—18th century
—History of doctrines—19th century
—History of doctrines—20th century
—History of doctrines—21st century
—Hot weather conditions *(May Subd Geog)*
—<u>Humor</u>
—Hurricane effects *(May Subd Geog)*
—Identification
—<u>Illustrations</u>
—<u>Indexes</u>
—Industrial applications *(May Subd Geog)*
—Influence
—Information resources
—Information resources management *(May Subd Geog)*
—Information services
—Information technology *(May Subd Geog)*
—Insignia

—Inspection *(May Subd Geog)*

—Installation *(May Subd Geog)*

—Instruments

—Interactive multimedia

—International cooperation

—Internet marketing *(May Subd Geog)*

—Interpretation

—Inventories

—Inventory control *(May Subd Geog)*

—Job descriptions *(May Subd Geog)*

—Juvenile drama

—Juvenile fiction

—Juvenile films

—Juvenile humor

—Juvenile literature

—Juvenile poetry

—Juvenile software

—Juvenile sound recordings

—Labeling *(May Subd Geog)*

—Labor productivity *(May Subd Geog)*

—Laboratory manuals

—Landscape architecture *(May Subd Geog)*

—Language

—Legends

—Library resources

—Licenses *(May Subd Geog)*

—Licenses—Fees *(May Subd Geog)*

—Lighting *(May Subd Geog)*

—Linear programming

—Literary collections

—Liturgy

—Liturgy—Texts

—Location *(May Subd Geog)*

—Longitudinal studies

—Maintenance and repair

—Management

—Manuscripts

—Manuscripts—Catalogs

—Manuscripts—Facsimiles

—Manuscripts—Indexes

—Manuscripts—Microform catalogs

—Maps

—Maps—Bibliography

—Maps—Early works to 1800

—Maps—Facsimiles

—Maps—Symbols

—Marketing

—Materials *(May Subd Geog)*

—Mathematical models

—Mathematics

—Measurement

—Medals *(May Subd Geog)*

—Medical examinations *(May Subd Geog)*

—Meditations

—Membership

—Methodology

—Microform catalogs

—Miscellanea

—Models *(May Subd Geog)*

—Moisture *(May Subd Geog)*

—Moral and ethical aspects *(May Subd Geog)*

—Museums *(May Subd Geog)*

—Mythology *(May Subd Geog)*

—Name

—Names

—Newspapers

—Noise

—Nomenclature

—Nomograms

—Notation

—Observations

—Observers' manuals

—Officials and employees

—On postage stamps

—On television

—Online chat groups

—Orbit

—Outlines, syllabi, etc.

—Packaging *(May Subd Geog)*

—Packing *(May Subd Geog)*

—Pamphlets

—Papal documents

—Parodies, imitations, etc.

—Passenger lists

—Patents

—Periodicals

—Periodicals—Abbreviations of titles

—Periodicals—Bibliography

—Periodicals—Bibliography—Catalogs

—Periodicals—Bibliography—Union lists

—Periodicals—Indexes

—Personal narratives—History and criticism

—Personnel management

—Philosophy

—Photographs

—Photographs from space

—Physiological aspects

—Physiological effect *(May Subd Geog)*

—Pictorial works

—Planning

—Poetry

—Political activity *(May Subd Geog)*

—Political aspects *(May Subd Geog)*

—Popular works

—Posters

—Power supply *(May Subd Geog)*

—Practice *(May Subd Geog)*

—Prayers and devotions

—Prayers and devotions—History and criticism

—Preservation *(May Subd Geog)*

—Press coverage *(May Subd Geog)*

—Prevention

—Prices *(May Subd Geog)*

—Prices—Government policy *(May Subd Geog)*

—Private collections *(May Subd Geog)*

—Privileges and immunities

—Problems, exercises, etc.

—Production and direction *(May Subd Geog)*

—Production control *(May Subd Geog)*

—Production standards *(May Subd Geog)*

—Programmed instruction

—Programming *(May Subd Geog)*

—Prophecies

—Protection *(May Subd Geog)*

—Provinces

—Psychological aspects

—Psychology

—Public opinion

—Public relations *(May Subd Geog)*

—Publishing *(May Subd Geog)*

—Purchasing *(May Subd Geog)*

—Quality control

—Quotations, maxims, etc.

—Qur'anic teaching

—Rates *(May Subd Geog)*

—Readings with music

—Records and correspondence

—Recreational use *(May Subd Geog)*

—Reference books

—Regional disparities

—Regions

—Registers

—Reliability

—Remodeling *(May Subd Geog)*

—Remodeling for other use *(May Subd Geog)*

—Remote sensing

—Repairing *(May Subd Geog)*

—Republics

—Research *(May Subd Geog)*

—Research grants *(May Subd Geog)*

—Reviews

—Risk assessment *(May Subd Geog)*

—Romances

—Rules

—Rules and practice

—Safety appliances *(May Subd Geog)*

—Safety measures

—Safety regulations *(May Subd Geog)*

—Sanitation *(May Subd Geog)*

—Scholarships, fellowships, etc. *(May Subd Geog)*

—Scientific applications *(May Subd Geog)*

—Security measures *(May Subd Geog)*

—Sermons

—Sermons—History and criticism

—Sex differences  *(May Subd Geog)*

—Signers

—Simulation games

—Simulation methods

—Slang

—Slides

—Social aspects  *(May Subd Geog)*

—Societies, etc.

—Sociological aspects

—Software

—Songs and music

—Songs and music—Discography

—Songs and music—History and criticism

—Songs and music—Texts

—Soundproofing  *(May Subd Geog)*

—Sources

—Specifications  *(May Subd Geog)*

—Specimens

—Spectra

—Speeches in Congress

—Stability

—Standards  *(May Subd Geog)*

—State supervision

—States

—Statistical methods

—Statistical services

—Statistics

—Storage  *(May Subd Geog)*

—Study and teaching  *(May Subd Geog)*

—Study and teaching—Activity programs  *(May Subd Geog)*

—Study and teaching—Audio-visual aids

—Study and teaching—Simulation methods

—Study and teaching—Supervision  *(May Subd Geog)*

—Study and teaching (Continuing education) *(May Subd Geog)*

—Study and teaching (Continuing education)—Audio-visual aids

—Study and teaching (Early childhood) *(May Subd Geog)*

—Study and teaching (Early childhood)—Activity programs  *(May Subd Geog)*

—Study and teaching (Early childhood)—Audio-visual aids

—Study and teaching (Elementary) *(May Subd Geog)*

—Study and teaching (Elementary)—Activity programs  *(May Subd Geog)*

—Study and teaching (Elementary)—Audio-visual aids

—Study and teaching (Elementary)—Simulation methods

—Study and teaching (Graduate) *(May Subd Geog)*

—Study and teaching (Higher) *(May Subd Geog)*

—Study and teaching (Higher)—Activity programs *(May Subd Geog)*

—Study and teaching (Higher)—Audio-visual aids

—Study and teaching (Higher)—Simulation methods

—Study and teaching (Internship) *(May Subd Geog)*

—Study and teaching (Middle school) *(May Subd Geog)*

—Study and teaching (Middle school)—Activity programs  *(May Subd Geog)*

—Study and teaching (Middle school)—Audio-visual aids

—Study and teaching (Preschool) *(May Subd Geog)*

—Study and teaching (Preschool)—Activity programs  *(May Subd Geog)*

—Study and teaching (Preschool)—Audio-visual aids

—Study and teaching (Primary) *(May Subd Geog)*

—Study and teaching (Primary)—Activity programs *(May Subd Geog)*

—Study and teaching (Primary)—Audio-visual aids

—Study and teaching (Residency) *(May Subd Geog)*

—Study and teaching (Secondary) *(May Subd Geog)*

—Study and teaching (Secondary)—Activity programs  *(May Subd Geog)*

—Study and teaching (Secondary)—Audio-visual aids

—Study and teaching (Secondary)—Simulation methods

—Study guides

—Tables

—Tables of contents

—Taxation *(May Subd Geog)*

—Taxation-Law and legislation *(May Subd Geog)*

—Technique

—Technological innovations *(May Subd Geog)*

—Telephone directories

—Terminology

—Terminology—Pronunciation

—Territories and possessions

—Testing

—Textbooks

—Texts

—Themes, motives

—Therapeutic use *(May Subd Geog)*

—Tombs *(May Subd Geog)*

—Toxicology *(May Subd Geog)*

—Trademarks

—Translating *(May Subd Geog)*

—Translations

—Translations into [name of language]

—Transportation *(May Subd Geog)*

—Tropical conditions

—Union lists

—Union territories

—Use studies

—Validity *(May Subd Geog)*

—Valuation *(May Subd Geog)*

—Vibration *(May Subd Geog)*

—Vocational guidance *(May Subd Geog)*

—Voivodeships

—Waste disposal *(May Subd Geog)*

—Waste minimization *(May Subd Geog)*

—Water-supply

—Web-based instruction *(May Subd Geog)*

—Weight

—Weights and measures

# Glossary

**aboutness** A term used to express those attributes of a resource concerned with its content, subject or topic, rather than its form. What a resource is 'about' forms the basis for subject cataloging. *See also* subject analysis

**abstract** *See* summary

**access point** A heading given to a catalog or database record or entry in a bibliography which enables a user to find the item

**Anglo-American Cataloguing Rules (AACR2)** A set of rules for descriptive cataloging adopted by libraries in English-speaking countries. Replaced by RDA (*Resource Description and Access*) in 2010

**authorized heading** *See* preferred term

**authority control** The control of access points by establishing and using consistent headings

**authority file** A collection of authority records containing the preferred forms of headings for names, series and subjects. *See also* Subject authority file

**authority record** A record of the preferred heading for a person, place, corporate body, series or title and the references to and from the heading. *See also* Subject authority record

**authority work** The establishment and maintenance of authority files

**bibliographic record** A catalog entry containing full cataloging information for a given item

**biography** 1. A written account of a person's life. 2. The branch of literature concerned with people's individual lives

**Boolean queries** Using the terms 'and', 'or', 'not' to formulate online search commands when searching LCSH in *Classification Web*

**Boolean operator** The terms 'and', 'or', 'not'. **And**: retrieves only items with both terms. **Or**: retrieves items with either term. **Not**: retrieves items with one term and not the other. These words are used in the formulation of search strategies for the retrieval of online information

**broader term, broader topic** BT. A more general subject heading

**BT** *See* broader term, broader topic

**catalog** A list of library materials contained in a collection, a library or a group of libraries, arranged according to some definite plan

**cataloger** A person who prepares catalog entries and maintains a catalog so that library materials can be retrieved efficiently

**cataloging** The preparation of bibliographic information for catalog records. Cataloging consists of descriptive cataloging, subject cataloging and classification

**cataloging-in-publication** CIP. Cataloging data produced by the national library or other agency of the country of publication, included in the work when it is published

**cataloging tools**  Publications of the international cataloging rules and standards, including *Resource description and access (RDA), Library of Congress subject headings (LCSH), Library of Congress classification (LCC), Dewey decimal classification (DDC)*

**chronological subdivision**  also period subdivision. A subdivision which shows the period or span of time covered by a work, or the period in which the work appeared

**CIP**  *See* cataloging-in-publication

**classification number**  Number allocated to a library item to indicate a subject

**Classification Web**  A Library of Congress subscription-based product that provides online access to LCSH and a number of other subject headings schemes, as well as to the Library of Congress Classification (LCC) scheme

**controlled vocabulary**  Predetermined terms chosen to represent concepts, found in an authoritative list of terms—e.g., Library of Congress Subject Headings, a database thesaurus

**corporate body**  An organization or group of people identified by a particular name, and acting as an entity

**correlation**  In *Classification Web*, the matching of a LCSH subject term to a classification number frequently used with that term, and vice versa

**cross-reference**  *See* reference

**database**  A collection of records, usually in machine-readable format, each record being the required information about one resource

**direct entry**  A heading using the specific term which describes the topic—e.g., Red fescue

**direct subdivision**  A subdivision which directly follows the main heading or subdivision. Usually used for geographic subdivisions. *See also* indirect subdivision

**foreword**  A brief statement of the reasons for the book, usually by the author or editor. It appears after the title page and before the introduction

**form**  1. The way in which a bibliographic work is arranged—e.g., dictionary. 2. Type of literary work—e.g., poetry, drama

**form heading**  A heading which represents the physical, bibliographic, artistic or literary form of a work—e.g., Encyclopedias, Dictionaries, Short stories. LC provides a separate list of genre/form subject headings. *See also* Genre heading; Library of Congress genre/form terms for library and archival materials (LCGFT)

**form subdivision**  A subdivision which brings out the form of a work—e.g., **—Periodicals**, **—Bibliography**

**free-floating subdivision**  A subdivision which may be used under any existing appropriate LC subject heading

**free text vocabulary**  *See* uncontrolled vocabulary

**general reference**  A reference made to a group of headings, rather than one specific heading—e.g., Woodworking industries—*SA names of specific industries, e.g.* Furniture industry and trade

**genre heading**  A heading which represents the category to which a resource belongs—e.g., fiction, horror films, bathymetric maps. LC provides a separate list of genre/form subject headings. *See also* Form heading; Library of Congress genre/form terms for library and archival materials (LCGFT)

**geographic heading**  Place name used as a subject heading. See also jurisdictional heading; non-jurisdictional heading

**geographic name**  Name of a place—country, state, city, town, suburb etc.

**geographic qualifier**  The name of a larger geographic entity added to a local place name or feature—e.g., Murg River (Germany)

**geographic subdivision**  Place name used as a subdivision of a topic

**hierarchy**  A system of organization in which narrower topics are part of broader topics

**homonym**  A word which sounds the same as another, and may be spelt the same, but has a different meaning

**index**  1. An alphabetical list of terms or topics in a work, usually found at the back. 2. A systematically arranged list which indicates the contents of a document or group of documents

**indirect subdivision**  A subdivision in which another element is interposed between the main heading and the specific subdivision. Usually used for geographic subdivisions. *See also* direct subdivision

**inverted heading**  A heading in which the normal order of the words is reversed, in order to group like terms together in the subject list—e.g., Cooking, French

**jurisdictional heading**  A geographic heading used for a political jurisdiction, that is the name of an area used to represent a government—e.g., 'Austria' rather than 'Republic of Austria'. *See also* non-jurisdictional heading

**keyword**  A significant term found in a document which identifies subject content

**LC**  *See* Library of Congress

**LCGFT**  *See* Library of Congress Genre/form Terms for Library and Archival Materials

**LCSH**  *See* Library of Congress Subject Headings

**Library of Congress**  The library of the United States Congress; the de facto national library of the United States

**Library of Congress Genre/Form Terms for Library and Archival Materials (LCGFT)**  A list of subject headings separate from LCSH, developed by the Library of Congress and used to indicate the style (genre, e.g., horror fiction) of a resource, or its format (form, e.g., map)

**Library of Congress Subject Headings**  The authoritative list of subject headings compiled and maintained by the Library of Congress

**Library of Congress Subject Headings Manual**  The Library of Congress' policies and instruction on using LCSH, to be used in conjunction with the LC subject headings scheme

**multiple subdivision**  A subdivision which is used to show the creation of similar subdivisions under the same heading, e.g., —Religious aspects—Buddhism, [Christianity, etc.]

**name authority file**  A collection of authority records containing the preferred forms of headings for names, including personal and corporate names

**narrower term, narrower topic**  NT. A more specific subject heading

**natural language**  *See* uncontrolled vocabulary

**non-jurisdictional heading**  A geographic heading used for a place other than a political jurisdiction—e.g., Great Barrier Reef, Hoover Dam. *See also* jurisdictional heading

**non-preferred term**  Also unauthorized heading. A term which is not taken from an authorized list of headings and should not be used. Usually a synonym for the preferred term

**NT**  *See* narrower term, narrower topic

**pattern heading**  A heading which serves as a model of subdivisions for headings in the same category—e.g., the pattern of subdivisions for 'Foot' can be followed for any similar part of the body

**period subdivision**  *See* chronological subdivision

**phrase heading**  A heading consisting of a group of words

**post-coordinate**  Of subject headings or other search terms, put together by the user at the time of searching

**pre-coordinate**  Of subject headings or other search terms, put together by the cataloger or indexer

**preface**  The author's or editor's reasons for the book. It appears after the title page and before the introduction

**preferred term**  Also authorized heading. A term taken from an authorized list of headings and used in a catalog

**qualifier**  An addition to a name etc. enclosed in parentheses

**reference**  A direction from one heading to another. *See also* see reference; see also reference

**related term, related topic**  RT. A subject heading at the same level of specificity to another heading and related in subject matter

**RT**  *See* related term, related topic

**SA**  *See* see also reference

**scan**  To examine a document for its main points, without reading the entire document

**scope note**  A note describing the range and meaning of a subject heading

**search term**  A word, phrase or number entered by a user to find the records on a database which match the term

**see also reference**  A direction from one heading to another when both are used

**see reference**  Also USE reference. A direction from one heading which is not used to another heading which is used

**skim**  To examine a document for its structure and an overview of its contents, without reading the entire document

**subdivision**  An extension of a subject heading which indicates an aspect—form, topic, place or period

**subject analysis** Identification of the intellectual content of a work; determining what a work is about. *See also* aboutness

**subject authority file** A file of all the subject headings used in the catalog, and the relevant references

**subject authority record** A record of a subject heading which shows the preferred form as well as notes on how this was derived, the authority used to determine the heading and the references to and from the heading in the catalog

**subject cataloging** Describing the content of a work using subject headings

**subject entry** An entry under the heading for the subject

**subject heading** A heading which describes a subject and provides subject access to a catalog

**Subject Headings Manual** *See* Library of Congress Subject Headings Manual

**summary** Also abstract. A brief statement of the essential points of an article or literary work

**synonym** A word with the same meaning as another

**thesaurus** 1. A work containing synonymous and related words and phrases, indicating the associations between them. 2. A list of controlled terms used in a database

**topical heading** A heading which represents a subject or topic

**topical subdivision** A subdivision which represents an aspect of the main subject other than form, period or place

**UF** *See* USED FOR reference

**unauthorized heading** *See* non-preferred term

**uncontrolled vocabulary** Also natural language, free text vocabulary. Terms taken directly from the work, without reference to a list of subject headings, thesaurus or authority file

**USED FOR reference** UF. The notation used with a preferred heading, which shows the non-preferred heading so that a *see* reference can be made—e.g., 'Capture at sea - UF Maritime capture' means that 'Capture at sea' is the preferred heading, not 'Maritime capture'

**USE reference** *See* see reference

**vocabulary control** Using the same terms all the time to indicate the same topic, by restricting the terms in a catalog, bibliography or index to those taken from a list of subject headings or thesaurus. *See also* controlled vocabulary; uncontrolled vocabulary

# Bibliography

Broughton, Vanda, *Essential Library of Congress subject headings,* London, Facet, 2012.

Chan, Lois Mai, *Library of Congress subject headings: principles and application* 4th ed., Westport, Conn., Libraries Unlimited, 2005.

Landry, P., Bultrini, L., O'Neill, E. T. & Roe, S. K. (eds.) (2011). *Subject access: preparing for the future,* Berlin, De Gruyter, 2011.

Langridge, D. W., *Subject analysis: principles and procedures*, London, Bowker-Saur, 1989.

Library of Congress, *Library of Congress subject headings,* various editions, Washington, D.C., Library of Congress.

Library of Congress, *Subject headings manual*, Washington, D.C., Library of Congress, continuously revised

Olson, Hope A. and John J. Boll, *Subject analysis in online catalogs* 2nd ed., Englewood, Colo., Libraries Unlimited, 2001.

Studwell, William E., *Library of Congress Subject Headings: philosophy, practice, and prospects,* Hoboken, N.J., Taylor & Francis, 2013

Svenonius, Elaine, *The intellectual foundation of information organization*, Boston, Mass., MIT, 2000

# Index

# LIBRARY SCIENCE TITLES

**LibrarySpeak:**
**A Glossary of Terms in Librarianship and Information Technology,**
International Edition ©2015
Lynn Farkas
**ISBN: 9781590954423** Paperback

**My Mentoring Diary:**
**A Resource for the Library and Information Professions**
Revised Edition ©2015
Ann Ritchie and Paul Genoni
**ISBN: 9781590954430** Paperback

**Quality in Library Service:**
**A Competency-Based Staff Training Program**
International Edition ©2015
Jennifer Burrell and Brad McGrath
**ISBN: 9781590954447** Paperback

**TOTALRECALL PUBLICATIONS, INC.**
1103 Middlecreek,
Friendswood, TX 77546-5448

**Phone:** (281) 992-3131
**email:** Sales@TotalRecallPress.com
**Online:** www.totalrecallpress.com